DOCTRINAL PREACHING
FOR TODAY

Andrew Watterson Blackwood

DOCTRINAL
PREACHING
FOR TODAY

CASE STUDIES OF BIBLE TEACHINGS

BAKER BOOK HOUSE
Grand Rapids, Michigan

© 1956 by Abingdon Press
Library of Congress Catalog Card
Number: 56-8739
ISBN: 0-8010-0638-4

First printing, July 1975
Second printing, November 1978

Paperback Edition
issued July 1975 by
Baker Book House
with permission of copyright owner

PHOTOLITHOPRINTED BY CUSHING - MALLOY, INC.
ANN ARBOR, MICHIGAN, UNITED STATES OF AMERICA
1978

THE PURPOSE
OF THIS BOOK

THIS BOOK ADVOCATES DOCTRINAL PREACHING BY THE local minister. The friend in view has been reading articles about "theology today," and hearing addresses on "religion in life." Sensing the needs of lay hearers, he wishes to preach doctrinal sermons. While keeping all his pulpit work inspirational, he would make a good deal of it informative. He faces a task both difficult and fascinating.

The book also recommends teaching the subject in schools of theology. As a rule seminary upperclassmen give doctrine a large place in their studies, but not in their sermons. If anyone asks why they do not preach more doctrine, they reply that no one has taught them how. Like their pastors at home, many students feel that professors ought to have taught them how to preach Christian doctrine for today. Little do they know about the difficulty of teaching the subject practically in the seminary.

These conditions have been changing for the better. Before World War II many pastors and students did not wish to preach doctrine. When I began teaching at Princeton Seminary, the curriculum exalted theology, both systematic and biblical. During the first month I was asked to read 360 sermons, 6 from every senior. After I had gone through the manuscripts, I said to one of the new friends: "In class you men devote to theology more time than to anything else. In

7

these sermons many of you preach well, but why does no one mention a Christian doctrine?"

"Surely," he answered, "you don't expect us to preach that stuff! It bores us stiff. Let us forget our theology and deliver inspiring sermons like we hear back home." Today in that seminary, as in most others, a typical senior or graduate student gives theology the first place in his thinking, and longs to do so in the pulpit. First he may have to learn how.

In quest of light one may go to a theological library. From scholarly books one can learn almost everything about doctrine except how to preach it. In a *Bibliography of Practical Theology*,[1] which I edited, a reader gets little help from the section entitled "Doctrinal Preaching." In other areas we compilers had to select and omit; for this part we could not find practical books. Every able writer on "What to Preach" had a good chapter on the theory of my subject, but no one had written a book about the use of doctrine in the pulpit. Since then the situation has changed little.

The first part of my book deals with theory, practically; the second part with application, still more practically. Much of the time I am breaking new ground. As in a book for doctors or lawyers, the project calls for case materials. Here they come from sermons, many of them from yesterday, and others from today, when such printed messages do not abound. Some cases deal with doctrine directly; others, indirectly. Both methods prove effective, if only for variety. "Never do anything all the time."

I have received encouragement and help from editors and librarians; and from graduate students, notably F. Leslie Conrad, S.T.M., Ronald E. Joiner, S.T.M., and Eugene N.

[1] (Princeton, N. J.: Theological Book Agency, 1949), 71 pp., paper, 50¢.

Patterson, Th.D. I feel grateful most of all for the Scriptures, from which we derive our Gospel. I hope that every reader will approach the book in the spirit of these words from an epistle full of inspired wisdom about the use of doctrine in the pulpit: "We preach not ourselves, but Christ Jesus the Lord; and ourselves your servants for Jesus' sake" (II Cor. 4:5).

ANDREW WATTERSON BLACKWOOD

CONTENTS

PART ONE

Meeting the Needs of the Hearers

PART TWO

Preparing a Doctrinal Sermon

CONTENTS

Meeting the Needs
of the Hearers

CHAPTER ONE

THE NEEDS
OF CHURCHGOERS

EVERY PASTOR KNOWS THE HEART HUNGER OF MEN AND women in his community. If any minister forgets, he can find surveys of laymen's needs, religiously. Instead of making another survey, I introduce three lay reporters. The first shows that there can be nothing new about the need for doctrinal sermons. The second reports conditions in Great Britain. The third tells about matters here at home. Anyone can cite other witnesses; these three show what lies back of the present book.

LISTENING TO LAY LEADERS

The first layman on the Yale Lectures brought *A Voice from the Crowd*. George W. Pepper, a lawyer, defined preaching as "the public use of speech with intent to reveal God to man," and a doctrinal sermon as "the Christian solution of a felt difficulty," not as "a complicated prescription for an unknown disorder." In a lecture about "Revelation Through Teaching," this layman referred to instruction as perhaps the chief agency of revelation, and "the basis of all good preaching." As for the need of pulpit doctrine, "in nine cases out of ten the man next me in the crowd, whether he is or is not an occasional church-goer, has an idea of God that is too hazy to be communicated." [1]

From Britain Dorothy L. Sayers reports conditions much

---

[1] (New Haven, Conn.: Yale University Press, 1915), pp. 33, 115.

the same. "Not one person in a hundred has the faintest idea what the Church teaches about God or man or society or the Person of Jesus Christ. If you think I am exaggerating, ask the army chaplain." This reporter used to send out thrilling mystery stories. Now she finds more drama in redemption, about which most laymen know nothing. Among them she points out three groups. "Frank and open pagans, whose notions of Christianity are a dreadful jumble of rags and tags of Bible anecdote and clotted mythological nonsense." "Ignorant Christians, who combine meek-gentle-Jesus sentimentality with humanistic ethics." "More or less instructed church-goers."

"If the churches are discredited today, it is not that they are bigoted about theology, but that they have run away from theology. The Church of Rome alone has retained her prestige, because she has put theology in the forefront of her teaching." [2] This analyst declares that the Protestant minister has a better opportunity for doctrinal preaching today than at any time for two hundred years. Laymen feel eager to hear a man with a message from God, if he knows how to speak in terms of today.

A third observer, C. Crane Brinton, is brilliant and scholarly. This Harvard professor of history deals with *The Shaping of the Modern Mind*. As proposed alternatives to Christianity, he studies humanism, rationalism, and Marxism. The philosopher of history reaches a conclusion that heartens a preacher of doctrine:

These impersonal faiths have little to offer the unhappy, the maladjusted, the suffering . . . nor do they offer the spiritual

[2] From *Creed or Chaos*, copyright 1949 by Dorothy L. Sayers.

security, the flexible discipline, that the Christian doctrine of sin and repentance offers. . . . The masses have never been able to take the tragic view without the help of a personal religion, a religion always hitherto transcendental, supernatural, otherworldly. . . . We human beings cling to certitude. Those who lost Christian certitude promptly tried to find scientific certitude, historical certitude, certitude anywhere they could turn it up. And we cling to omniscience as the companion to certitude.

Where else can laymen find it, Brinton asks, if not in "the old, consoling religions"? [8]

Men and women everywhere keep groping after God. They turn to religious books, some of which become best sellers, with the Bible always in the lead. In a recent year, so the American Bible Society reports, almost ten million North Americans purchased various versions of the Scriptures. Not one buyer in ten may know how to read the Book. These facts afford every pastor a rare opportunity, which will not last. If a purchaser does not learn how to read his Bible, he will lay it on a shelf with his New Year's resolutions, to gather dust.

Such readers also feel perplexed about modern works on religion. Even the best books for laymen, as by C. S. Lewis, may not help a man ignorant of the Bible. A seeker after God asked a dealer to send him forty religious books, which the businessman and his wife started to read. After a while he told her that they would understand these books better if they began with the Bible. Through a pastor they learned to read the Book, doctrinally. Soon they became Christians, active in service. "Understandest thou what thou readest?" asked a Christian worker of a prominent stranger. "How can I, except some man should guide me?" (Acts 8:30c, 31a.) In the Greek the word "guide" means to "lead along the way."

[8] (New York: New American Library, 1954), pp. 252-55.

LEARNING FROM OTHER CHURCHES

In these matters we can learn much from Roman Catholics. By television, printed matter, and countless other means they strive to win recruits, always on the basis of doctrine. Among intelligentsia, farmers, and city Negroes the ways of appeal differ widely. An inquirer can always find an expert ready to teach Roman Catholic doctrine. As for the results of such propaganda, opinions differ widely. Probably they lose to us many more recruits than they gain among nominal Protestants. Not so among city Negroes. One of their local city pastors wonders why Protestant churches practice "segregation on Sunday," and why we let Roman Catholics win Negroes, who hold the balance of power, politically, in our country:

The blame for this rapid and increasing trend toward Roman Catholicism does not rest solely with churches composed of white people; it can be laid also to the ineffectiveness of Negro Protestantism. The Negro ministry has relied too largely on emotionalism, and has failed to stress the teaching function of the Christian ministry. Many Negroes join the Roman Catholic Church because they believe it gives them a doctrinal foundation for their religious living. They have not chosen between Catholic doctrine and Protestant doctrine, but between Roman dogma and nothing.[4]

With a few changes this account would show what many a white congregation gets from the pulpit. Doctrinally, next to nothing! Instead of assailing Roman Catholics, why do we not teach our people the doctrines of the Reformation? If our members become concerned about Roman Catholicism, they will welcome messages about "The Rule of Faith," the basis of authority in religion. In a church bulletin the texts below

[4] Reuben L. Speaks, "Will the Negro Remain Protestant?" *The Christian Century*, June 2, 1954, pp. 668-69.

might not appear, as the teaching does not depend on a few isolated texts. The topics refer to four successive sermons. Everything centers in the authority of Christ.

THE SUPREME AUTHORITY AMONG PROTESTANTS

The Authority of Christ as Teacher—Matt. 7:28-29
The Authority of Christ as Master—Matt. 28:19-20
The Authority of Christ as Comforter—John 14:1-2
The Authority of Christ as Judge—II Cor. 5:10a

Protestants believe that "Christianity is Christ," not the Church. If we learn the will of God in Christ, through the Spirit, we have the decisive word on what to believe, how to live, and what to hope for. Often we say the same thing by insisting on Holy Scripture as "the only infallible rule of faith and practice." This I believe with all my heart, but I feel that the pulpit stress ought to fall on the authority of Christ. If my account makes the facts seem simple, that is what a pastor must do in presenting doctrine to lay hearers. Make clear that this teaching comes from God, and they will see that it is better than Roman teaching about the authority of the Church. With Protestants, as with the New Testament, the authority of Christ

Rests in a Divine Person, Not an Institution;
Relies on Divine Principles, Not Human Rules;
Refers to Believing Persons, Not Special Priests;
Rejoices in God's Love, Not Human Laws.

Pastors can also learn much from newer bodies that have sprung up among Protestants. What Elton Trueblood reports about his home town, Richmond, Indiana, is often duplicated elsewhere. Older churches are marking time; newer bodies are growing in numbers and power. Two such groups head the national lists for per capita giving, denominationally. As for the secret of growth, these bodies rely largely on preaching, especially the preaching of doctrine. They give a large place to eschatology. In personal work and in other ways they seem to be "always abounding in the work of the Lord." This account calls for no endorsement of certain "fringe groups." Some of the "newer churches," such as that of Father Divine, may not even be Christian. Still we can learn much from the best of the newer bodies.

INTRODUCING MEN TO GOD

Laymen have a right to expect doctrinal preaching. Many of them want it, and others will respond after they get accustomed to "new" pulpit diet. "As if increase of appetite had grown by what it fed on." If pastors knew what their laymen want, there would be much doctrine from the pulpit. An able book on Preaching, by Walter R. Bowie, says that more than a hundred young married people were asked to choose among twenty-four subjects the ones they thought most vital for them personally. In this homemade "Gallup Poll" they put first these two subjects: "Some Trends in Modern Theological Thinking" and "What Is the Christian Interpretation of Death?" Both subjects doctrinal and one of them eschatological! If you were the pastor, handing out a list of twenty-four assorted subjects, would you expect more than one hundred young married people to choose these two?

These lay folk must know that their minister can preach on difficult subjects. They would not relish the stuff we often dish out as "pulpit doctrine." They wish a man to know what he is talking about, to present a subject with absorbing interest, and to show what difference it ought to make in home and office. They have no time for dry-as-dust disquisitions about "the

Infinite, Eternal, and Unchangeable, with His attributes of omniscience, omnipotence, omnipresence, and transcendence." In thought-forms of our day every one of these abstractions would ring a bell in the hearts of young married church people. They think of life in terms of persons, in action, full of struggle and suspense, often shadowed by fear of the unknown morrow.

I am thinking of my own first attempts in this difficult field. My experience resembled that of a gifted minister whom I now quote, but I had never enjoyed "good training in homiletics." This ought to include training in how to meet the needs of men by preaching the truths of God. Partly because of my early experience, I believe that professors of homiletics in the past must bear much of the blame for the paucity of doctrinal preaching today. Homiletics ought to mean more than assorting dry bones dug up from an abandoned burial ground. Now hear the witness:

My first sermons were hardly models of their kind. It was not that I lacked good training in homiletics, but because I had so little time for preparation, and the sermons were steeped in theological language, they seemed unreal. Once, when I had preached on "The Ontological Argument for the Proof of the Existence of God," Mrs. Ella Bullock, a devout and motherly deacon, called me to her home the next day and said, "Son, we don't need all that theology, philosophy, and psychology. We need some 'peopleology,' and 'Negro-ology.' Talk about something we know. Help us to live, young man." With a kindly laugh she added, "Talk about something you know something about, too."
I accepted the advice gratefully.[5]

The sister gave her minister better advice about homiletics

[5] From *Road Without Turning*. The Story of Reverend James H. Robinson. Copyright 1950 by James H. Robinson. Published by Farrar, Straus and Cudahy, Inc.

23

than many of us received in the seminary. Still we wonder about her assumption that a pastor ought to eschew theology. Should he not rather make each doctrine glow with an inner light from God? At Harvard a brilliant lecturer on the Ingersoll Foundation spoke about the hereafter as it appears in Negro spirituals.[6] No congregation would find this kind of doctrine dry.

There would be more preaching of doctrine if professors cut short their exhortations and turned their students loose in a theological library to ferret out doctrinal sermons, good and bad. "Badness" here refers to form, not content; we are not engaged in a heresy hunt. As an example of badness, through ignoring human needs, turn to an able preacher of yesterday. He is speaking about "Providence," with no boundary lines. Wisely he starts with a text about persons. Joseph is speaking to his older brothers: "As for you, ye thought evil against me; but God meant it unto good" (Gen. 50:20).

After a conventional introduction the preacher developed five headings.

   I. By the Providence of God I mean that preserving and controlling superintendence which he exercises over all the operations of the physical universe, and all the actions of moral agents.
  II. The Providence of God is universal, having respect to every atom of creation and every incident of life.
 III. This universal Providence is carried on in harmony with . . . those modes of operation which we call natural laws.
  IV. God's Providence is carried on for moral and religious ends.
   V. The Providence of God contemplates the highest good of those who are on the side of holiness and truth.[7]

[6] See Howard Thurman, The Negro Spiritual Speaks of Life and Death (New York: Harper & Bros., 1947).
[7] William M. Taylor, The Limitations of Life and Other Sermons (Manchester: James Robinson, 1899), pp. 249-63.

Admirable ideas, ponderously expressed! Or rather, shipped by slow freight! The dear man could have shown how the providence of God worked among the sons of Jacob, and among the friends in the pews at Broadway Tabernacle. The dominie forgot that providence has no meaning apart from persons, divine and human. This is the sort of doctrinal preaching many students were taught to admire and imitate. Fortunately, professors today have rediscovered the Bible way of revealing the truth of God in His dealings with men. This way calls for facts, facts, facts, about persons in action, often dramatic. Such facts emerge near the end of the sermon. Though not ideal in form, this illustration stands out like an oasis in a desert of dreary abstractions:

In the ancient city of Chester [England] . . . there is an old building . . . having these words engraved on the lintel of the door: "God's Providence is mine inheritance." It is said that when the plague last visited the city, that was the only house which escaped the visitation, and so its inmates sculptured these words upon it as a record of their gratitude.

MAKING DOCTRINE PERSONAL

Some preachers can make this doctrine seem personal and practical. In Toronto during World War I, Robert Law delivered a sermon about "The Providence of God in the Fall of a Sparrow" (Luke 12:6). Better still, after that conflict Arthur J. Gossip of Glasgow started with a subject sure to attract attention: "How to Face Life with Steady Eyes." This man chose a royal text: "God is our refuge and strength" (Ps. 46:1). His opening words had to do with his hearers, weary of war. Here follows a part of the introduction, full of facts, tense with drama, all about persons:

25

That long line of fires of burning homesteads and the like crept ever nearer as blaze after blaze shot up; the women . . . with their fingers always twitching nervously about their lips although their eyes were tearless; the men speaking low, because already fear was knocking at their hearts. A few hours more, and these invincible armies would be coiled chokingly about the little town. And then, God pity us, what then? Everywhere there were consternation, and confusion, and despair. . . .

Among it all this man moved calm, and cool, and unafraid. Why? Life had taught him to know God, and he trusted Him absolutely even then. "Aren't you forgetting God?" he asked the scared and shuddering groups. And yet when did He ever fail us?

A little later the Scottish interpreter declares: "That is one of the differences that religion makes." Not all the sermon moves on the same high level, for at times the hearer needs relief from the increasing tension. Near the end the interpreter returns to his original motif and asks: "Aren't you forgetting God?" All this about "How to Face Life with Steady Eyes." Then the preacher quotes what Luther wrote to Melanchthon:

From the bottom of my heart I am against those worrying cares which are taking the heart out of you. Why make God a liar in not believing His wonderful promises, when He commands us to be of good cheer, and cast all our care upon Him, for He will sustain us? Do you think He throws such words to the winds? What more can the devil do than slay us? Christ has died for sin once for all, but for righteousness and truth He will not die, but live and reign. Why then worry, seeing He is at the helm? He who has been our Father will also be the Father of our children. As for me . . . , I do not torment myself about such matters.[8]

Another interpreter has brought strength and hope through a message about "The Gospel of the Sovereignty." At Bourne-

---

[8] *The Hero in Thy Soul* (New York: Charles Scribner's Sons, 1930), pp. 91-92, 104-5. Used by permission of the publisher.

mouth, a resort on the English Channel, J. D. Jones used this subject in preaching about contrasting texts. After an old-fashioned introduction, partly unnecessary and far too long, he brought out two contrasting truths:

I. The Gospel and Holy Awe: "The Lord reigneth; let the people tremble" (Ps. 99:1).
II. The Gospel and Holy Confidence: "The Lord reigneth; let the people rejoice" (Ps. 97:1).

I prefer the order of the ideas as they appear in the "royal psalms." I should deal with the Holy Confidence before the Holy Awe, putting the ideal before the opposite, the light before the shadow. Still I like the body of this sermon, which bases a good man's life on his understanding of God.[9]

More recently James S. Stewart of Edinburgh preached the same truth, with even more relation to the hearer's needs. With no reference to the sovereignty of God, the interpreter dealt with this truth as it shone out from his text: "The Lord God omnipotent reigneth" (Rev. 19:6), a text that served as the topic. The message began with a kind word to the hearer —an introduction that shows how to start religiously, with absorbing interest.

The body of the message consists of three parts. At first one asks about the order of the parts. Perhaps the interpreter wished to begin with what would interest the hearer. Then he led up to a truth that would throw light on the vast beyond. This message has a sturdy framework, but does not follow stereotyped rules. Here follow the three main headings, like the piers in a suspension bridge, planned to take every hearer Godward.

"First, the liberation of life." "A sense of absolute release."

[9] The Gospel of the Sovereignty (London: Hodder & Stoughton, Ltd., 1915), pp. 1-17.

27

Release "from petty worries"—"fears of life"—"self-contempt." Second, *the doom of sin.* "The ultimate defeat of evil in every shape or form. . . . No one was ever so sure of this as Jesus. . . . Fight on, then, you who have lost heart because your own conflict is so difficult, your tempter so strong and dogged and subtle. Fight on! 'The Lord God omnipotent reigneth!' " "Third, *the comfort of sorrow.*" Here the speaker deals triumphantly with the floods of life, notably the flood we know as Calvary. "The Lord sat as King at the Flood."

Do you believe it? My friend, here is surely the final victory of faith—to be able to say, "The Lord God omnipotent reigneth," to cry it aloud, not only when life is kind and tender and smiling, and the time of the singing of birds is come and the flowers appear on the earth, but even more when the night is dark and you are far from home, and the proud waters are going over your soul; to cry it then, not weakly nor diffidently nor uncertainly, but vehemently and passionately and with the ring of faith in every syllable of it—"The Lord God omnipotent reigneth." [10]

These examples show that a minister can use Christian doctrine in meeting the needs of his hearers. Also that two interpreters, starting with the same Bible teaching, at the same time in history, can use a doctrine in ways as different as the Epistle to the Romans differs from First Peter. In the pulpit the stress ought to fall, not on explaining a doctrine, but on meeting a need, and that by preaching a truth from God.

[10] *The Gates of New Life* (New York: Charles Scribner's Sons, 1940), pp. 11-20. Used by permission of the publisher.

CHAPTER TWO

THE RETURN
TO DOCTRINAL PREACHING

S OME CHURCH HISTORIAN OUGHT TO TRACE THE RISE
and fall of doctrinal preaching through the centuries. Such
pulpit work tends to flourish, or languish, according to the ebb
and flow of spiritual life in the Church. When prophets and
apostles, or Luther and Calvin, preached doctrine, the Church
made an impact on the age. In what Kenneth S. Latourette
terms "The Great Century," the nineteenth, the foremost
pulpit masters relied largely on doctrine. Such preaching declined during the first half of the twentieth century. So did
the influence of the Church and the clergy. Of late there has
been a "theological renaissance" in our seminaries; and there
will be one soon, I hope, in our pulpits.

TURNING AWAY FROM DOCTRINE

The turning away from pulpit doctrine appears in two
collections of sermons, each by a skillful compiler. In 1908
Grenville Kleiser sent out ten little volumes, *The World's
Great Sermons*, most of them from the nineteenth century.
Among the 113 selections, more than half seem to me doctrinal. In recent years G. Paul Butler has compiled series of *Best
Sermons*, most of them excellent. The volume before me has
fifty-two brief sermons, few of them doctrinal. Another reporter
might count differently, as such labels cannot be exact. No
student of the two series could question the change from the
preaching of doctrine in the time of Spurgeon and Moody to

the custom of doing something else during the first part of the twentieth century.

Charles H. Spurgeon represented his time. One of his early volumes, typical of many, has twenty-seven sermons, more than half of them doctrinal. Canon H. P. Liddon of St. Paul's appeals more to some of my friends. One of his volumes has forty-two discourses, at least half of them doctrinal. Six concern the hereafter, including his famous discourse "The First Five Minutes After Death" (I Cor. 13:12). On our side of the Atlantic doctrine abounds in the printed sermons of Bushnell, Brooks, Beecher, and many others of yesterday.

The inclusion of Henry Ward Beecher may seem strange. One of his ministerial admirers, Newell D. Hillis, went through Beecher's published works and other sermon manuscripts, and reported:

> Once in three years he made the round of Christian truth and experience, preaching on the great epochs of the spiritual life, and on the great themes, the Scriptures, God, Christ, the Holy Spirit, man, his dignity, his need, his ignorance and sinfulness, the nature and number and order of the spiritual faculties, the method of quickening in men a sense of sin, the nurture of faith, the development of love, the feeding the hope of the life of man.[1]

APPRAISING RECENT SUBSTITUTES

About the turn of the century men who issued books of sermons began to include fewer doctrinal messages. As early as 1905 a gifted evangelical liberal, Charles E. Jefferson, warned his brethren against the neglect of doctrine in the pulpit.

> [A man] can give his sermon the Christian atmosphere and let a stream of Christian sentiment trickle through its paragraphs . . .

[1] Lyman Abbott et al., *Henry Ward Beecher as His Friends Saw Him* (Boston: Pilgrim Press, 1904), p. 27.

without even so much as once referring to those fundamental dogmas by which the church of God lifted the Roman Empire off its hinges, and turned the stream of the centuries into a new channel. . . . Applied Christianity has been our theme; but alas, we have had too little Christianity to apply. . . . Moreover, the new preaching of Christianity with Christian dogma eliminated does not seem to be working well.[2]

During the succeeding generation preachers tried all sorts of substitutes for doctrinal sermons. I have watched many such experiments, often appreciatively. I believe that many of these methods have a place in the Church, but never as substitutes for pulpit doctrine. Enriched worship—religious education—religious drama—audio-visual methods—the social gospel—the problem approach—the life-situation sermon—the case method—the symphonic sermon—and pastoral counseling. With one or two exceptions, which of these methods calls for a question mark? But these ways of doing God's work ought not to interfere with preaching the doctrines of redeeming grace. Woe to the Church if methodology ever serves as a pulpit substitute for what scholars call the kerygma, or preaching the Gospel.

The "theological renaissance" has been spreading from divinity schools to pastors' studies. Every well-informed pastor knows more or less about "What Present-Day Theologians Are Thinking." Instead of merely reading secondhand accounts of their books, a wise man gets to know writings from such men as Aulén, Baillie (Donald and John), Barth, Berkhof, Brunner, Buber, Bultmann, Calhoun, Chafer, Cullmann, DeWolf, Dillistone, Ferré, Horton, Hunter, Lewis (C.S. and Edwin), Mackay, Maritain, Niebuhr (Reinhold and Richard),

[2] *The Minister as Prophet* (New York: T. Y. Crowell & Co., 1905), ch. v, "The Place of Dogma in Preaching."

Nygren, Shaw, Taylor, Temple, Tillich, and Whale. No one would care equally for the writings of all these men; surely I do not. Every minister ought to know that these men have been writing and that their books are being read.

Without admiring much that W. Somerset Maugham has written, I welcome these words as a code for a minister: "No reading is worth while unless you enjoy it. . . . I am not a scholar, a student, or a critic. I am a professional writer, and I now read only what is profitable to me professionally." In like manner a pastor may resolve: "I shall read only what will in time help me to preach, and I shall preach on no vital subject about which I have not read." [3]

Every pastor ought to know the books of C. S. Lewis, if only because his way of presenting doctrine appeals to many laymen. From England this brilliant university professor sends out lay sermons that fascinate the "untheologically minded." For example, in three terse sentences he sets forth the heart of New Testament teaching about the Final Return of our Lord:

    I. Christ will certainly return.
    II. We cannot possibly find out when.
    III. Therefore we should always be ready for Him.[4]

LEARNING TO DO BY DOING

Any minister who enjoys reading theology will soon feel a desire to share the new visions with his people. He may hold back because he does not know how to preach doctrine. Perhaps not, but he can learn. He may have been delighted with a scholarly monograph about *The Body: A Study in Pauline Theology.* "The concept of the body forms the keystone of

[3] *The Summing Up* (New York: New American Library, 1954), p. 60.
[4] *Eternity Magazine*, March, 1954, p. 10.

Paul's theology." [5] Can this be correct? The author shows that from the sins of the body we are set free; through the body of Christ we are saved; to His body, the Church, we belong; through His body, in the Eucharist, we are blessed; in the body we now show new life; in the body we shall share the resurrection. "Here, with the exception of the doctrine of God, are represented all the main tenets of the Christian faith —the doctrines of Man, Sin, the Incarnation, the Atonement, the Church, the Sacraments, Sanctification, and Eschatology."

What an opening for a sermon, or better still, later on, a series! Nothing interests a typical layman more than his body. He may not yet be ready for a doctrinal series, but he will relish a sermon on a subject that most pulpits have neglected: "Religion for a Man's Body." By reading up on the subject, and by preparing to preach such a sermon, a pastor will learn more about this kind of pulpit work than he can learn in any other way. He will also have the satisfaction of finding that his first doctrinal sermon has fostered a desire for "more of these practical talks that help us laymen live."

The text may come from Romans. After eleven chapters of doctrine, the Apostle makes an application. Knowing that the readers are exposed to all the bodily allurements of a pagan city, he starts the practical exhortations with a plea for the Christian use of their bodies. "I beseech you therefore, brethren, by the mercies of God, that ye present your bodies a living sacrifice" (Rom. 12:1). What pastor does not sense the need of such teaching in the home community today? Why not follow Paul's example and base it frankly on doctrine? Topic: "The Christian Use of Your Body."

[5] John A. T. Robinson (London: Student Christian Movement Press, 1952), p. 9.

33

The sermon may fall into three main parts:

I. An act of Christian worship, a sort of burnt offering. A burnt offering was entirely consumed. God wants your body as a whole and in every part.

II. A way of Christian living. God wants your body to be "holy," a word close to another term, "healthy." "Acceptable to God" means that He wishes to have in His service the best body you can give.

III. A glimpse of the Christian reason. Why? Because God has done so much for you in the body of Christ on the Cross.

"Is this what you mean by a doctrinal sermon?" Yes, in one of myriad forms. Throughout this book the stress will fall on the pulpit use of one doctrine after another as a God-given way of meeting heart needs of men and women. Hence the discussion will have more to do with preaching as the interpretation of life today than with systematic theology as it appears in some learned books. On the other hand, more than a few theological writers of today present gospel truth in such attractive forms that the pastor can learn from them how to preach, as well as what to say.

A doctrinal sermon ought to consist of something far more substantial than a string of stories. Still the truth in hand may require an example or two from the workaday world. For example, take the use of tobacco. The majority of ministers feel that this is neither an unpardonable sin nor an appointed means of grace. The use of the weed does not show that a man is headed for hell, just as abstinence does not ensure him a safe conduct to heaven. God is far more vitally concerned about "weightier matters of the law, judgment, mercy, and faith."

The Bible says nothing about the use of tobacco, which white men seem not to have known before 1492. Still the Apostle's teaching about the body has a bearing on the question "Shall I smoke or not smoke?" The biography of the late Chief Justice Hughes tells about his concern for the efficiency of his body. After he had reached middle age, he gave up two habits in which he had indulged all through manhood. He quit doing hard mental work after dark, and he gave up the use of tobacco. As an earnest Baptist layman, his religious beliefs no doubt influenced this latter decision. The biographer, presenting the facts on the basis of physical and mental efficiency, quotes the Chief Justice: "Giving up smoking improved my health and increased my efficiency twenty-five per cent."[6] That seems like a large dividend from such an investment.

After Albert Einstein had passed middle age, he quit smoking. In earlier years, whenever we saw him at his home in Princeton, we found him with his pipe in his mouth. When last we called to bid him farewell, and to thank him for many kindnesses, we saw that he no longer played with his pipe. He explained that after he had had a serious operation, followed by more or less continuous pain, the physician had suggested cutting down the use of tobacco. "No," said the scientist, "if tobacco is not good for my body, I must give up my pipe." The doctor told him that this was not necessary, but the man of science insisted on doing what was best for his body. According to reports in reputable magazines, President Eisenhower came to a like conclusion after he had arrived at middle age.

A man in the pulpit has no more right to forbid a layman's smoking than a layman has to frown on his pastor's Monday morning game of golf. But the minister has the God-given privilege of teaching the layman to use his body according to the will of his Lord. If the minister dealt with such matters on the sole basis of ipse dixit, the layman might feel affronted,

* Merlo J. Pusey, *Charles Evans Hughes* (New York: The Macmillan Co., 1951), I, 299.

and justly so. But if the minister can show that both the soul and the body of the believer belong to God, then the interpreter has a right to ask that the custodian of the Lord's body take first-class care of this priceless body, which does not really belong to him. As for the practical application of the truth, the minister must leave all that with the layman and his Lord.

SECURING WHOLESOME VARIETY

Does the return to doctrinal preaching mean that a pastor ought gradually to quit preparing sermons of other kinds? Should he cease to inspire, and change his pulpit into a professor's desk for teaching theology? God forbid! Every church needs both inspirational sermons and informative messages. Every minister ought to preach both ways. A doctrinal sermon, ideally, should be so full of life, motion, and color that only the most thoughtful laymen will discover that they are hearing doctrine. Even so, if a man always strives to inspire, he may lose his appeal. On the other hand, if he always tries to teach, his pulpit work may savor of needless sameness.

If I were still a pastor, as I am at heart, I should think in terms of fifty-fifty. Instead of trying to make half of each sermon informative and the other half inspirational, I should deliberately plan to make a particular sermon as uplifting as possible, and to make another one as informative as the facts warranted. If on every Lord's Day I had two regular services, as I did for seventeen happy years, I should strive to make the morning message inspirational, with a certain amount of teaching. I should wish to capture the boys and girls, and others young in heart, so that in the beauty of life's morning they would form the habit of enjoying church attendance and public worship, which includes preaching.

At night, with ways of worship less formal, I should have some sort of teaching message, as a rule doctrinal. I believe that almost every community includes more than a few men and women who would welcome the right sort of doctrinal sermons at night. If it did not seem feasible to have a second service, I should divide my pulpit ministry about fifty-fifty, according to the season. Meanwhile, if I may judge from sermons that appear in print, at least 95 per cent of American sermons must be of the inspirational type and less than 5 per cent doctrinal.

The preaching of our time often excels in human interest. Since Bible days the work of the pulpit may never have been so interesting as now. May the sermons of tomorrow prove to be equally inspiring. May they also excel in a more difficult respect, that of teaching men what to believe. What Phillips Brooks told young men at Yale still holds true: "Preach doctrine, preach all the doctrine that you know, and learn forever more and more; but preach it always, not that men may believe it, but that men may be saved by believing it." [7]

Gerald Kennedy shows how to do such preaching today. He starts with a life situation concerning an outcaste woman of India toiling in a paddy field under a scorching sun. "Tell me," says a visiting divine from England, "what can a woman like that understand about Christianity?" "She knows," replies a missionary, "that Christ is stronger than the demons." The rest of the brief introduction puts a question in terms of an ignorant man here at home. How can a friend in the pew tell him about Christ? The answer comes from Paul, who "faced this problem many times and he became a master at finding the door to men's understanding and need." The topic seems

[7] Lectures on Preaching (Grand Rapids, Mich.: Zondervan Publishing House, 1950), p. 129. Used by permission of the publisher.

to me admirable; so does the sermon as I have seen it in outline.[8] I omit some of the bishop's short comments.

THE ABC OF THE GOSPEL

"I am not ashamed of the gospel: it is the power of God for salvation to every one who has faith" (Rom. 1:16 R.S.V.).

I. We must always begin with the certainty that
Every Man Is a Sinner.

II. The second proposition follows from the first; namely,
Every Man Needs a Saviour.

III. The third proposition is that
The Saviour Is Jesus Christ.

[8] *Pulpit Digest*, Aug., 1955, p. 26.

CHAPTER THREE

THE PREACHING
OF DOCTRINE INDIRECTLY

MINISTERS PREACH DOCTRINE IN VARIOUS WAYS, NOTA-
bly two. Men of yesterday, such as Robert William
Dale, of Birmingham, often did it directly. Men of today,
such as James S. Stewart, sometimes do it indirectly. They follow the maxim of F. W. Robertson at Brighton: "Preach
suggestively, not exhaustively." The case for the indirect
method appears in a strong book by Harold A. Bosley, *Preaching on Controversial Issues*. He discusses Communism and
other live issues. In what follows I have made the application
to doctrinal preaching, a field that Bosley's book does not
enter.

Instead of "strumming a single string on his homiletical in-
strument," says Bosley, a pastor ought to employ both the
direct and the indirect approach—that is, one or the other in a
given sermon.

The indirect approach is used more frequently by most preachers,
I should assume, and with good cause. As a rule, it begins with
some great religious theme—like faith or humility—and develops its meaning in terms of Scripture and Christian history.
Then with this as a firm foundation, the preacher is able to move
with freedom and decision among the vital problems of his own
day illustrating the meaning, the power, and the need of such
virtues or beliefs now. This approach wears well, and it ought to be
the main one used by any preacher today as it has been through the
centuries.[1]

[1] (New York: Harper & Bros., 1953), pp. 21-22. Used by permission of
the publisher.

In the next few chapters we shall think about preaching doctrine indirectly. In naming a sermon, in making an approach, and in developing a message, such an interpreter does not stress the doctrine, but uses it to meet human needs. Let no one think of the indirect method as evasive or cowardly. Each exemplar who follows believes in the Trinity with all his heart. He regards himself as a popular interpreter of this truth with reference to human needs, not as a classroom lecturer on doctrine for its own sake.

PREACHING ABOUT THE TRINITY

In Unitarian Boston for twenty-four years (1869-93) Phillips Brooks preached doctrine indirectly. In his ten volumes of sermons delivered there, at least half of the two hundred seem to me doctrinal, indirectly. Often Brooks dealt with the truth enshrined in the name of "Trinity Church." Not controversially or apologetically, but joyously and persuasively, he led men to look on the Trinity as "the description of what we know about God," as "the center and circumference of our faith," as "a truth for every Lord's Day and all of life."

This doctrine is not "a puzzle or a satisfaction to the intellect, but an expression of the manifold helpfulness with which the divine nature offers itself to the human." "If a man does believe the doctrine of the Trinity, he ought to rejoice and glory in his faith as the enrichment of his life. Not as a burden on his back, but as wings to his shoulders, he ought to carry his belief." These excerpts from sermons by Brooks accord with his Yale Lectures on Preaching: "I should count any Sunday's work unfitly done in which the Trinity was not the burden of our preaching." Brooks did not speak as a theologian. He added little to our knowledge of the truth that undergirds all our other beliefs.

James S. Stewart presents the same doctrine indirectly. In his volume *The Strong Name* [2] all the messages have to do with the Trinity. Few of them afford explanations of the truth at hand. The first nine have to do with "The Grace of the Lord Jesus Christ"; the next seven, "The Love of God"; and seven more, "The Communion of the Holy Ghost." The last section includes sermons about truths indirectly related to the Spirit. As in a classic novel, the closing message shows the dominant purpose of the artist. Here Stewart preaches about the "Apostolic Benediction" (II Cor. 13:14). As in the other parts of the book, he deals with the fact of the Trinity suggestively, not exhaustively.

In evangelical churches the same truth rings out from every standard hymnal. A first-class hymn means Christian doctrine set to music. In some books the table of contents begins with hymns about the Trinity—Father, Son, and Holy Spirit. These hymns come mainly from other times, when holy men of song thought much about God. One who wishes to preach about the Trinity indirectly may follow the stanzas of a well-known hymn which has sturdy structure. Passing by Heber's majestic words "Holy, holy, holy!" one finds it easier to deal with a less exalted hymn, "Come, Thou Almighty King." One may ask the people to keep the hymnbooks open at this place, and at an evening service, if local custom permits, have them read in unison the four stanzas, at intervals. The sermon takes for granted that men worship no one but God.

THE TRINITY IN HOLY SONG

Like many another hymn, a prayer to God
   I. We pray to God the Father.
   II. We sing praises to God the Son.

[2] New York: Charles Scribner's Sons, 1941.

III. We adore God the Spirit.
IV. We worship the blest Three in One.
The Lord inspired the song; He waits to bless the singer.

This message proves nothing and explains little. The Bible never "proves" the fact of the Trinity or explains the meaning. Why should we attempt to do so? We might as well "prove" and "explain" light and life and love. Not by thinking but by experience do the children of God enter into holy mysteries. As Pascal used to say, "The heart has its reasons, which reason does not know." A boy or girl of ten or twelve can worship God the Father, the Son, and the Spirit so as to feel "lost in wonder, love, and praise." This idea of the Trinity stands out in a poem by Heinrich Heine:

> Ah, my child, while yet I nestled
>   In my mother's lap and love,
> I believed in God the Father,
>   Good and great, who reigns above. . . .
>
> Then, my child, as I grew bigger,
>   Things I mastered, more than one;
> I began to use my reason,
>   And believed in God the Son. . . .
>
> Now that I have grown to manhood,
>   Read and travelled more than most,
> Swells my heart, and I acknowledge
>   With full heart the Holy Ghost.[3]

DEALING WITH A BENEDICTION

The indirect method lends itself to preaching about a Bible benediction. A person should do this more than once, but at intervals, for benedictions do not come in clusters. The first message ought to make clear that we mean by a benediction

[3] Kate Freiligrath Kroeker, ed., *Poems Selected from Heinrich Heine* (London: Walter Scott, Ltd., 1904), p. 145, "A Mountain Idyl."

42

God's way of blessing people assembled in His presence. A benediction differs from a prayer. In a public prayer a minister speaks to God on behalf of men. In a benediction he pronounces the blessing of God on men with hearts open to receive His grace. If a minister occasionally uses his hands when calling men to pray, he lifts the hands up with palms toward heaven, symbolizing angels of God ascending. In a benediction he always lifts both hands aloft, with palms toward the people, to symbolize angels descending.

A sermon about a benediction ought to show the importance of this act in worship. Nothing else a minister does for God should loom larger in the eyes of the people. Many of them regard the benediction as merely a sign that the service has ended and that they can make ready to go home. They would attach more importance to the act if the minister always did his part correctly. Instead of conveying the blessing of God, he sometimes starts with the weak word "may," thus changing a benediction into a prayer. Why ask God to do what He is waiting to do? No man can "improve" the form of a Bible benediction.

THE BEST OF ALL BENEDICTIONS (II Cor. 13:14)

The benediction as the summit in public worship
  I. The best thing about Jesus Christ—His Grace
      Grace brought Him to earth—led Him to the Cross—comes from Him now.
  II. The best thing about God the Father—His Love
      Love chooses us as children—redeems us from sin—transforms us into saints.
  III. The best thing about the Holy Spirit—His Communion
      Fellowship brings us close to God—imparts to us His peace—enables us to do His will.
By faith receive this benediction.

Unless a man knows how to paint with a large brush, the message will seem crowded. One could have a series of three sermons, but why not preach about the benediction as a whole? Once I did so. Twenty years later I asked which of my sermons I should publish, and my wife referred to this one, which I had forgotten. She did not recall the sermon so much as the benediction. Neither did she refer to the doctrine, for the message dealt with the Trinity indirectly.

People will feel grateful for a sermon about "The Benediction of God's Peace": "The God of peace . . . make you perfect" (Heb. 13:20, 21). One day two high-school teachers, about to embark on a sabbatical year abroad, asked me to use this benediction the last time they attended the home church. They love this benediction best of all, and so do I. Many prefer one that grows out of Phil. 4:7: "The peace of God, which passeth all understanding, keep your hearts and minds in the knowledge and love of God, and of His Son, Jesus Christ our Lord; and the blessing of God Almighty, the Father, the Son, and Holy Spirit, be amongst you, and remain with you always. Amen." As a subject James S. Stewart uses this: "When God's Peace Guards the Door."

Sometime preach about "The Most Beautiful Benediction." Without irreverence employ plural pronouns. In public worship a benediction conveys God's blessing to a throng as a whole: "The Lord bless you, and keep you: the Lord make his face shine upon you, and be gracious unto you: the Lord lift up his countenance upon you, and give you peace" (Num. 6: 24-26). These words full of beauty come out of a background seemingly as dreary as a desert, in a manual for Hebrew priests. A minister can look at the words in light that streams from the New Testament. He need not show what they meant when they first fell on the desert air, but what they should mean to believers now. Whenever he utters these beautiful words of blessing, the people ought through faith to receive threefold blessings from heaven:

    I. Loving care from God the Father
   II. Light from the living Christ
  III. Peace from the Holy Spirit

EXPLAINING HOLY BAPTISM

The words used in baptism afford an opportunity to preach the same doctrine, indirectly. According to a leading Episcopal bishop the New Testament says more about baptism than about the Lord's Supper. People ought to know about baptism, which lies at the heart of New Testament Christianity. The meaning appears in the Great Commission, which says in part: "Go ye therefore, and teach all nations, baptizing them in the name of the Father, and of the Son, and of the Holy Ghost" (Matt. 28:19). The act of baptism assumes the reality of "God in Three Persons, blessed Trinity."

The spirit of these words appears in a treatise by Augustine, bishop of Hippo (d. 430). In *De Trinitate* he declares: "O Lord, our God, we believe in Thee, the Father, the Son, and the Spirit. For the Truth would not say, 'Go baptize in the name of Him who is not the Lord God.'" What a mockery if either pastor or people thought of the Father alone as completely divine, of the Son as partially so, and of the Spirit as a sort of religious electricity! "God in Three Persons"!

In preparing such a message decide what to stress. Emphasize the truth about the Trinity, or the meaning of baptism. People who come to church know more about baptism than about the Trinity. Begin with them where they are, religiously. Then proceed to what they need to know about God. By relating baptism to the Trinity you can show the bearing of this doctrine on Christian experience. Otherwise a message about the Trinity might seem as cold, hard, and lifeless as the wrong sort of old-time classroom monologue about dogmatic theology.

In administering this rite a pastor says to a candidate: "I baptize thee in the name." Everyone ought to understand that "name" here means "person," or "character." If worthy to receive baptism, the candidate belongs to God as heavenly Father, to Christ as Lord and Master, to the Spirit as Counselor and Guide. Baptism also means that through the Holy Spirit this person publicly professes his faith in Christ as his Saviour from sin, and his desire to become a member of the local church.

In a backward tribe of Central Europe the meaning of baptism used to appear dramatically. In the presence of his tribesmen the new convert would stand facing the East and solemnly declare: "I accept Thee, O Christ, as my Saviour and King. I shall serve Thee alone, forevermore." Turning to the West, he would say: "I renounce thee, O Satan, and all thy works. Henceforth I shall serve thee no more, forever." What an impressive way for a man to approach baptism!

Like the Lord's Supper, baptism sets forth the drama of redemption. Hence boys and girls ought to witness both these memorable events. Albert Schweitzer attributes his missionary zeal partly to the way he as a little lad used to watch his loved ones commune. So did the leading proponent of the social gospel remember most clearly from boyhood days the impressiveness of baptism. Walter Rauschenbusch loved to recall those dramatic scenes because they appealed to his imagination.[4]

---

[4] See Dores R. Sharpe, *Walter Rauschenbusch* (New York: The Macmillan Co., 1942), p. 35.

LEADING UP TO COMMUNION

Preaching doctrine indirectly also applies to the Lord's Supper. By explaining this rite a minister can set forth the world's most wondrous drama. In churches that celebrate the Communion at intervals, the meditation before the Sacrament need not be long or heavy. There is not time, nor is this the place, for a thoroughgoing exposition of the doctrines involved. The minister should lift every heart up to God. How can he do this better than by dealing with some one aspect of the Lord's Supper?

A brief meditation, devotional, not didactic, provides an opportunity to discuss a chosen aspect of truth that makes the Communion precious to the redeemed. In the New Testament every passage about the Lord's Supper relates it to Christ. One aspect relates to the Christ of yesterday and one to the Christ of tomorrow. All the rest, at least eight, refer to "The Christ of Christian Experience," here and now. We come to meet with Him at His Table, not to mourn over Him at His tomb. Not in any material sense, we Protestants believe in the "Real Presence" of our Lord.

A pastor may remain with a congregation nine or ten years. At intervals he can deal with distinctive aspects of the Lord's Supper, one aspect in a message. (1) "A Memorial of the Cross": "This do in remembrance of me" (I Cor. 11:24c). (2) "A Symbol of Freedom from Sin," with a passage about "remission of sins" (Matt. 26:28). In a sanctuary where I serve in summer, when I present the people's gifts, I stand facing the altar. While we all sing the Doxology, I can see myself reflected in the Cross. So whenever one serves as "His hand with which He gives needy souls the bread that is His body," one's disloyalties come home to roost. One's sins never seem so ghastly as at His Table or at His Altar, where one seems to soil

47

the vessels with one's touch and fears lest one block the flow of redeeming grace.[5]

(3) " A Meal with Guests of God," from a text about the Passover as a family meal (Luke 22:14). (4) From the same text or one like it speak about "The Round Table of Christ." According to well-known legends the noblest British king gathered about him a band of loyal knights, sometimes twelve and again a larger throng. Before King Arthur sent them out on "deeds of bold emprise," he ate with them at a round table where everyone could see and hear the king. So with a motto text look on the round table as a symbol of fellowship. This word, the koinonia, means enjoying what we have in common with Christ and His soldiers.

I. Fellowship with Christ as King
II. Fellowship with knights of the King
III. Fellowship with those who have fallen in battle
IV. Fellowship in preparation for service
    "Lead on, O King Eternal,
      The day of march has come."

Other meditations deal with the response of those who commune in faith. These messages may prove more difficult to prepare. (5) "A Covenant with Christ as King": "This cup is the new covenant in my blood" (I Cor. 11:25b R.S.V.). A covenant means God's way of choosing us as children and our way of accepting Him as Father through Christ and His Cross. On another level, dear to many hearts, a bride says at the marriage altar: "I do promise and covenant." According to Eichrodt and other biblical theologians the Covenant stands at the heart of our holy faith.

(6) A like word, Sacrament, comes from the Latin, where

---

[5] Two sentences almost verbatim from A. J. Gossip, *In Christ's Stead* (New York: George H. Doran Co., 1925), p. 41.

it means an oath of allegiance to the emperor. At baptism a recruit for Christ's army puts on the uniform of Christ as King. At the Communion he ratifies this oath of allegiance. If anyone prefers a softer word, he may speak of a "vow." As in a marriage service, a vow consists of words to be kept sacred, whatever the cost. This line of thought about the Sacrament may not stand out in any text, but the call for loyalty to Christ rings out everywhere in the New Testament.

(7) Another note sounds from the Words of Institution: "As often as ye eat this bread, and drink this cup, ye do shew the Lord's death till he come" (I Cor. 11:26). In the Greek this word "shew" usually means "proclaim," or "preach." Without violence to facts one can speak about "The Sermon in the Supper." (8) At another time one can single out the closing part of the same verse: "Ye do shew the Lord's death till he come": "The Lord's Supper and the Second Coming." So it seems that meditations about the Communion begin with looking back to "survey the wondrous cross," and lead on to a view of His coming in glory. We rejoice in His presence with us now, tender to sympathize, mighty to save. In the Presbyterian *Book of Common Worship* the following versicles lead up to the Eucharistic Prayer. All of this is optional:

> Minister: Lift up your hearts.
> People: *We lift them up unto the Lord.*
> Minister: Let us give thanks unto the Lord our God.
> People: *It is meet and right so to do.*

Sometime, not immediately before a Communion feast, sound a note of warning about "The Cause of Spiritual Anemia": "For this cause many are weak and sickly among you" (I Cor. 11:30). For what cause? Through not understanding the connection between the Lord's Supper and the Cross. To eat and to drink in an unworthy manner, says Paul, means to be "guilty of the body and blood of the Lord." So the Apostle bids believers examine their hearts to feel sure of trust in Christ and His redeeming grace. Then let them come to His Table and find "refreshing and rest unto [their] souls."

I may seem to ignore friends in bodies that hold other theories about sacraments and ordinances. Later I shall discuss such matters, kindly, I trust. Here I only urge that every pastor teach members of the home church what they should believe about baptism and the Lord's Supper. In content such pulpit teaching ought to be doctrinal. In form the teaching may be indirect, calling little attention to doctrine. In view of our lofty privilege as Christ's interpreters let us now unite in a historic prayer:

O God, who by the life and death and rising again of Thy dear Son hast consecrated for us a new and living way into the holiest of all; cleanse our minds, we beseech Thee, by the inspiration of Thy Holy Spirit, that, drawing near unto Thee with a pure heart and conscience undefiled, we may receive these Thy gifts without sin, and worthily magnify Thy holy Name; through Jesus Christ our Lord.[6]

* Liturgy of St. James, second century, A.D.

CHAPTER FOUR

THE DOCTRINE IN
SOUL-WINNING SERMONS

THE INDIRECT WAY OF PREACHING DOCTRINE LENDS itself admirably to pulpit evangelism. An evangelistic sermon brings the unsaved or unchurched hearer face to face with Jesus Christ and moves the hearer to accept Him as Saviour and Lord. Soul-winning sermons assume many forms, but such things as the distinction between evangelism and revivals need not concern us now. We ought rather to agree with C. H. Dodd [1] and other New Testament scholars who stress the kerygma, which means preaching the heart of the Gospel. This calls for doctrine. It often appears indirectly, not because of concealment or evasion, but because the sermon calls for acceptance of Christ, not merely for belief in a truth about Him.

In the past every evangelistic movement blessed of God has come largely through preaching doctrine. Evangelism has flourished, or languished, according to the amount and the fervor of such pulpit work. A book by James Burns, one of the ablest works in the field, refers to the great doctrines which in the different centuries have awakened men to newness of life. Every revival, therefore, is a return to Christ. It arises from a fresh recognition of His power to save the sinner awakened to a new consciousness of his sin, and to

---

[1] *The Apostolic Preaching and Its Developments* (London: Hodder & Stoughton, Ltd., 1949).

lead him into a new life of blessedness and peace with God.[2]

LOOKING TO FORMER EVANGELISTS

This book deals with the subject biographically. Burns uses six exemplars: Francis of Assisi, Savonarola, Luther, Calvin, Knox, and Wesley. The author might have included Bunyan and Baxter, Whitefield and Edwards, Finney and Moody, with others whose names the reader can supply. Some of them we admire more than others. From any of them we can learn the importance of basing soul-winning sermons on doctrine and of using it as a means of grace, not as an end in itself.

These soul winners have often preached doctrine indirectly. An English admirer of John Wesley has published an appraisal of him as a preacher.[3] The author shows that Wesley put first the preaching of "fundamental doctrines"; second, what the writer calls "speculative theology"; third, "miscellaneous sermons, dealing with matters of morals, expediency, and general decency." As an evangelist Wesley usually preached doctrine, often indirectly. In addressing believers he preached less doctrinally.

Much the same applied to Dwight L. Moody. In all his platform work, except near the end, he stressed the mercy of God. In his last tour of Britain—according to R. W. Dale, a friendly observer—Moody pleaded with men to do good and pay their debts. Dale reported that Moody continued to attract vast throngs, but did not have so many converts or do so much good as earlier when he relied on the saving

[2] *Revivals, Their Laws and Leaders* (London: Hodder & Stoughton, Ltd., 1919).
[3] W. L. Doughty, *John Wesley: Preacher* (Chicago: Alec R. Allenson, Inc., 1955), ch. ix, "John Wesley's Subjects."

truths of the gospel. An excerpt from Moody will show how he preached doctrine indirectly. In a passage that has become famous he represented Peter as asking: "Lord, do you really mean that we shall preach the gospel to every creature?"

Yes, Peter. . . . Go, search out the man who spat in my face; tell him that I forgive him; that there is nothing in my heart but love for him. Go, search out the man who put the cruel crown of thorns on my brow; tell him that I have a crown ready for him in my kingdom, if he will accept salvation. . . . Go, search out the soldier who drove the spear into my side; tell him that there is a nearer way to my heart than that. Tell him that I forgive him freely, and that I will make him a soldier of the Cross, and my banner over him shall be love.[4]

A generation after Moody, Walter A. Maier preached much the same gospel, doctrinally, but in a fashion more rugged. Over the radio he may have addressed more people in a single year than Moody did in ten. Moody's friendly approach pleased some observers more than the ways of Maier, but he too can teach us much. In the title of almost every volume he includes the name of Christ. In the book at hand every sermon seems to me doctrinal, at least indirectly. For example, take "Marred Lives," with a text concerning the house of the potter (Jer. 18:4). Maier begins with facts about the Patent Office in Washington and forty thousand inventions the preceding year. He insists that no one has discovered a human way to remake marred souls.

Like F. W. Robertson in this respect, Maier planned a sermon with two main divisions:

I. We have all been marred by sin.
II. We all can be remade in Christ.

⁴ Daniel A. Poling, ed., A Treasury of Great Sermons (New York: Greenberg, 1944), p. 118.

The closing paragraph tells about a manufacturer who heard a brilliant sermon by his pastor. The layman expressed admiration and then said: "If you were my salesman I would discharge you. You got my attention by your appearance, voice, and manner. Your prayer and logical presentation aroused my interest. You warmed my heart with a desire for what you presented. And then—you stopped without asking me to do anything about it. In my business the important thing is to get them to sign on the dotted line." [5]

LEARNING FROM RECENT EXPERTS

After World War I mass evangelism suffered a decline in favor. Now it has begun to come back. In Bryan Green, a British Anglican, it finds a winsome advocate. In his book *The Practice of Evangelism* one of the best chapters deals with "Evangelistic Preaching." He bases everything on the kerygma, the preaching of Christian doctrine. He also allows a lesser place to the didache, pulpit teaching not doctrinal or evangelistic. In putting the kerygma first, Green follows the apostolic preaching, about which C. H. Dodd and others have written ably.

Similar testimony comes from Charles B. Templeton. In Toronto he served most effectively as a self-taught evangelist. Then he came to Princeton Seminary to put a foundation under his faith. At my request he has prepared a statement setting up an ideal to which few have attained. This friend writes well:

There can be no evangelistic preaching not doctrinal, any more than there can be a skyscraper without girders, or a body without bones. There is a God-given connection between creed and deed.

[5] *He Will Abundantly Pardon* (St. Louis: Concordia Publishing House, 1948), pp. 79-101.

Men do according to what they believe. At least in part, Christians believe what they hear from the pulpit. The scandal of our times is that doctrinaire Communists believe their teachings more strongly than many of us believe our creeds. It is not enough for a preacher to inspire. Inspiration without teaching leads to frustration. The hearer must be led to a definite response, or he will be like Stephen Leacock's man who leaped on his horse and galloped away in all directions at once. There can be no reckoning of the hurt from so-called evangelism directed only at the emotions. The response can be only partial and the commitment temporary. We must preach a total gospel to a total man in a total life situation. The appeal must be to the mind and the emotions, the conscience and the will.

Two other men, each with a Southern Baptist background, have been making a tremendous impression. In South America, especially in Argentina, Tommy Hicks seems to have created a sensation, about which we in the United States know too little. Here and in Europe, Billy Graham has become far better known. His volume *Peace with God* shows that he believes in making pulpit evangelism doctrinal. He might not agree about the wisdom of doing it indirectly, but he never has seemed belligerent. His work has impressed me favorably for many reasons, not least because he refrains from throwing stones at other Christian leaders.

Graham's book falls into three parts, all doctrinal:

  I. The Problem (six sermons)
 II. The Solution (six)
III. The Result (six)

He starts with three assumptions: the hearer's past is full of sin; his present is sad because of frustration and defeat; his future looks dark because he faces death. Graham preaches today what Spurgeon did two generations ago. Like Spurgeon, he has a message full of hope. Without closing his eyes to the woes of men and the plight of the nations, he appeals most of all to one hearer on the basis of Christian truth:

God is still on the throne and in command of everything. . . . God has a definite plan for each period of history, for every nation and for every individual. The Scripture discloses God's plan for the return of Christ when His kingdom shall be established. . . . Thus, for the Christian, life has a plan and an assurance that God will ultimately triumph over all unrighteousness.

This excerpt shows that Graham does not strive to become known as a great preacher and philosopher. He wishes everyone to know that he has a great Gospel and a great God. His closing sermon, "Peace—At Last," shows a sense of beauty that does not often appear elsewhere, and a desire to bring peace to troubled hearts. These words compare favorably with the writing of men who find fault with the style of Graham's sermons:

The storm was raging. The sea was beating against the rocks in huge, dashing waves. The lightning was flashing, the thunder was roaring, the wind was blowing, but the little bird was asleep in the crevice of the rock, its head serenely under its wing, sound asleep. That is peace: to be able to sleep in the storm!
In Christ we are relaxed and at peace in the midst of the confusions, bewilderments, and perplexities of this life. The storm rages, but our hearts are at rest. We have found peace—at last! [6]

The evangelists I have cited differ from one another as much as the writers of the four Gospels. These later soul winners would agree that every community ought to hear such preaching, and that "professional evangelists" cannot meet the need. Every such man worth his salt would tell the local

[6] From: *Peace with God* by Billy Graham. Copyright 1953 by Billy Graham, reprinted by permission of Doubleday & Company, Inc.

pastor: "Do not imitate me, or anybody else. If you ape one of us, you will fail. Be yourself. Preach your way. In the local community soul winning depends largely on your preaching of doctrine and your ability to lead lay men and women in doing personal work." Amen! According to Francis Thompson

> There is no expeditious road
> To pack and label men for God,
> And save them by the barrel-load.[7]

SERVING AS A LOCAL EVANGELIST

"The pastor his own evangelist!" With some such motto a man becomes the leader of a soul-winning people. He may not start a crusade with the blaring of trumpets. He may not even plan a series and advertise it as evangelistic. If inexperienced he may have to prepare one soul-winning sermon at a time, until he gradually learns how. Since many persons today keep thinking about religion, he may start here. In answer to a question about the meaning of a man's religion, our Lord replied in terms of love. In preparing to preach from this passage, one may find the first main part difficult, the second less so, and the third least of all. Still he does well not to "improve" the order of Christ's words. Text: "Thou shalt love" (Matt. 22:37a).

THE MEANING OF A MAN'S RELIGION

A live question. Our Lord's answer in terms of love.
  I. Religion consists in loving God supremely.
 II. Religion calls for loving your neighbor largely.
III. Religion leads to loving yourself last.
Find this love and religion at the Cross, here and now.

[7] From "Epilogue, a Judgment in Heaven." Copyright by Sir Francis Meynell and used by permission of Burns Oates & Washbourne, Ltd.

Another sermon takes up the question "What do you mean by sin?" A seeker after God does not need a dictionary definition or a doctrinal disquisition. He may feel concerned about the sin of the world, but he finds it easier to think about the sins in himself. The text may come from our Lord's parable about a young man who went wrong. "When he came to himself," he said to his father, "I have sinned." (Luke 15: 17, 21.) In an expository sermon one would proceed differently. At present the aim calls for a simple statement of what sin means in the experience of a person today:

   I. A man's way of getting wrong with God
  II. Getting wrong with others
 III. Getting wrong inside himself

In a soul-winning sermon a minister ought to keep everything simple. He might discuss the saying of William James that a man feels "consciously wrong, inferior, unhappy." True, but the Bible relates sin to God. Religion begins with loving God supremely; sin consists in failing or refusing to do so. Sin against God leads to wrong relations with others, and to a wrong sort of inner self. If not in terms of the prodigal, somehow get the hearer to see himself as he stands in the eyes of God. From beginning to end deal with sin as a matter involving persons, human and divine. Pray that the end may be peace with God, and victory. If anyone prefers to preach about Christ, that is what I mean, "God in Christ."

In another sermon the approach may come through a Bible teaching about sin as a disease of the soul. The soul means one's inner self, what one is while alone in the dark. When a thoughtful person comes to church, you need not prove that something is wrong inside him. Assume that he knows more about sickness than about sin. Then remember the saying of an old book, not brilliant but full of leads for sermons: religion is "a remedy to be applied to the conscience rather than . . . a system of truth to be accepted by the reason." [8]

SIN—THE WORST OF ALL DISEASES

"With his stripes we are healed" (Isa. 53:5c).
I. Sin means sickness in a man's soul.
II. Such a sickness leads to soul death.
III. This sickness defies any earthly cure.
IV. Soul sickness calls for the healing Cross.
Christ waits here with His healing Cross.

This line of thought may help to answer another question: "What do you mean by being saved?" No one figure and no one sermon can explain all the facts, or take away the mystery. Without mystery a man's preaching would become a muddle. Even so, deal with salvation in terms of being set free from the deadly disease of the soul. God's way of setting a man free! As free as if one has contracted pneumonia and lies struggling for breath when all at once penicillin starts to work and sets him free. His anguish fades; his fears subside; his way back to health and strength lies open. The healing of a man's soul may follow another course, but it should lead to freedom from disease in the soul. "Earth has no sorrows that heaven cannot heal," right here and now. Text, the same as above (Isa. 53:5c).

I. Salvation means being set free from soul sickness.
II. Salvation comes through trusting the divine Physician.
III. Salvation brings strength to serve among men.
IV. Salvation waits for you at the healing Cross.

This sort of preaching relies largely on repetition. When

[8] W. Mackintosh Mackay, The Disease and Remedy of Sin (New York: George H. Doran Co., 1919), p. 1.

you talk to a man about what concerns his deepest self, you can repeat the same ideas again and again, each time perhaps in a new form. The element of variety may come through study of a case. Take the jailer at Philippi. In despair he cries: "What must I do to be saved?" The truth rings out, not in the question, but in the answer. The reply of the Apostle does not contain an abstract, impersonal word or idea; and neither should the sermon. "Believe on the Lord Jesus Christ, and thou shalt be saved" (Acts 16:31).

"This Business of Being Saved"
"What must I do?" "Be saved"—God does it through Christ.
  I. God's way of making you right with Himself
 II. His way of making you right with everyone else
III. His way of making you right inside yourself
God's way leads to the foot of the Cross. Follow His way!

With another question the answer may prove harder to state: "What does it mean to believe in Christ?" "I trust my wife, I depend on my physician, I rely on my banker, but still I have a sense of wrongness in my soul. What more can I do?" Here again one might use learned terms to perplex and bewilder an able man who knows next to nothing about spiritual anatomy and hygiene. Still you can keep him thinking about soul sickness and healing.

> Be of sin the double cure,
> Cleanse me from its guilt and power.

"How? What can I do in order to believe?"

The Meaning of a Man's Faith
  I. Knowing Christ as able to set one free
 II. Wanting to have this experience now
III. Putting oneself in His pierced hands
IV. Accepting the freedom He waits to bestow

Still the mystery remains. No one can understand how the divine Physician applies the healing balm and sets a mortal free from wrongness in his soul. One thing we know: the prescription always works. For a case study turn again to the Philippian jailer. Note the change in him, a man of middle age. A few hours ago he was beating innocent men and putting them in the stocks, with no salve for their bleeding backs. Before morning dawns, he has found the Saviour and has begun to serve others. In finding the Lord and Master this man has found himself (Acts 16:25-34). So may it prove with many a man, strong-willed, in your community. What does he need so much as an interpreter like Paul, showing him how to be saved?

AVOIDING COMMON PITFALLS

We have seen that a soul-winning sermon ought to have at its heart a Christian doctrine, and that the doctrine may appear indirectly, so that the hearer will think of his sins and his Saviour. Instead of following this trail, let us look at mistakes common in evangelistic preaching. For a vicious caricature we might turn to *Elmer Gantry* (1927), a novel by Sinclair Lewis. He holds up to ridicule a professional revivalist, self-seeking, money-loving, woman-seducing. Let us rather consider pitfalls that await a man of honor, a pastor who desires to win souls for the glory of the Redeemer. These matters seem self-evident, so they call for little comment.

1. *Emotionalism.* Emotion has its place. Without feeling there could be no soul winning. But there is also need for thought. The prophet was writing about sin when he said in the name of God: "Come now, and let us reason together" (Isa. 1:18a). From that time to this, excessive emotionalism

has often brought the Lord's business into disrepute.[9] Remedy: At the heart of every soul-winning sermon have a Christian doctrine.

2. *Traditionalism.* Almost every religious group has a number of stock phrases that have lost their pristine luster. In order to be counted orthodox, a minister feels that he must speak in these ways. To young people who think in terms of today his sermons seem unreal. I am not recommending any departure from the "faith of our grandmothers," but I feel that every man ought to dress his sermonic children in thought-forms of his own day. Remedy: As a preacher of doctrine follow the Golden Rule.

3. *Professionalism.* The wrong sort of revivalism fosters censoriousness, dogmatism, and an appearance of "superficial omniscience." A ministry that starts as a pilgrimage of faith may degenerate into love of money, thirst for approval, and striving after notoriety. Remedy: Keep close to Christian doctrine as it centers in the Christ of experience.

4. *Vagueness.* "Come to Jesus" means coming to Jesus, and "Believe on Christ" means believing on Christ. If at first the hearer does not understand, say it again and louder. Remedy: Become an intelligent interpreter of doctrine.

5. *Shallowness.* A "gospel sermon," so-called, may consist of exhortation, faultfinding, and bombast. Remedy: A study of Christian doctrine.

6. *Anecdotage.* Evangelistic preaching has become associated with sickly stories, improbable, impossible, unthinkable. To make up for mediocrity in quality, a man multiplies the number. He might as well expect a hatch of chickens from a setting of stale eggs. Remedy: Always state your truth and

---

[9] See F. M. Davenport, *Primitive Traits in Religious Revivals* (New York: The Macmillan Co., 1910).

make it clear. Then be sure that the illustration belongs on the same high level as the sermon.

7. *Monotony.* From week to week and from the beginning to the end of every sermon, no "surprise power." Remedy: Like Bunyan, learn to teach doctrine imaginatively.

8. *Speaking.* In other days revivalism called for excited utterance, excessive speed, and increasing shrillness. What an atmosphere to result in a decision for time and eternity! Fortunately, this kind of speaking has become outmoded. Most of us in the pulpit now seem tame. Remedy: A heart on fire with divine truth, and a longing to set other hearts aflame.

9. *Unpreparedness.* When a man has not time to prepare a sermon, he may substitute a "simple gospel talk." Later the devotee of "simple simplicity" tries it again. He may form the habit of "going everywhere preaching the gospel." Remedy: A determination to make every soul-winning sermon doctrinal, at least indirectly.

10. *Lack of prayer.* "Lord, teach us to pray!"

As an example of a soul-winning appeal that shows careful preparation, take the closing words of a sermon by Clovis G. Chappell. He has been preaching about "A Glimpse of the After Life" (Luke 16:19-31, a parable about "a certain rich man"). Note here the kind attitude, the directness, the clarity, the parallel sentences, the repetition, and the positive truth. No hearer should fail to understand or fail to respond. Read the excerpt aloud, with a clear, low voice. Read slowly, so that every word will leave its mark.

God has no way of getting any man into heaven when he has hell in his own heart. . . . Hell, whatever else it may be, is the burying ground of dead souls, souls that are dead in trespasses and in sin. . . .

Forever you are going to live. Forever you are going to be yourself. You are going to have to keep house with yourself for all eternity. Forever you are going to remember. Forever you are going to enjoy or suffer the destiny that you make for yourself while in this life. . . .

Remember, too, that though some men are lost, no man needs to be lost. Every man can be saved if he will. This minute you can be saved if you will only be wise enough and brave enough to make a right choice. "Him that cometh unto me I will in no wise cast out." Will you come? Will you come now? [10]

[10] *The Village Tragedy and Other Sermons* (New York and Nashville: Abingdon Press, 1925), pp. 90-91. Used by permission of the publisher.

64

CHAPTER FIVE

THE DOCTRINE
IN PULPIT COUNSELING

PREACHING IS PERSONAL COUNSELING ON A GROUP BASIS —nothing else."[1] So says Harry Emerson Fosdick, who for years engaged in such a pulpit ministry. At first his utterance may sound strange, but not after a person has thought about the history of preaching. When has a well-rounded ministry ever refrained from pulpit counseling? How else could anyone preach about the key verse in Pss. 42 and 43: "Why art thou cast down, O my soul?" In other days we called such sermons "pastoral preaching," because the minister tried to help believers in Christ. In our time with its increasing tensions there is double need for such preaching. So let us take for granted that in the pulpit nothing except soul winning ought to loom larger than Christian counseling.

A discussion of counseling might lead us far afield. Let us think about only one aspect: the need for basing all such counseling indirectly on Christian doctrine. In Paul's letter to the Philippians, as elsewhere, he tried to meet the heart needs of Christian friends, and always on the basis of doctrine. "In Christ!" To him the present "cult of reassurance" would have sounded as strange as it does to many of us who regard Paul as the chief interpreter of Christian faith and duty.

---

[1] Gertrude Samuels, "Fosdick at 75—Still a Rebel," New York Times Magazine, May 24, 1953, p. 14.

REFERRING EVERYTHING TO GOD

Preachers well grounded in doctrine form the habit of referring everything to God. In his years of retirement, for example, A. J. Gossip was asked to prepare a devotional book for use in Lent. He chose to write about prayer, with nine chapters that might have been counseling sermons.[2] In each case he answered a practical question on the basis of a Christian doctrine. The opening chapter, "Our Real Trouble; and Its Cure," shows the need for communion with God. The next study, "The First Law of Prayer," deals with "practicing the presence of God." So in part after part he leads up to a closing discussion: "On Some Methods of Prayer." No chapter without its doctrine, and no doctrine without a bearing on some human need. Everywhere here he uses doctrine indirectly.

Younger men have done much the same thing, but not in Gossip's way. Robert E. Luccock has a volume of sermons, *If God Be for Us*.[3] These words point to a doctrine that undergirds the book: "If God be for us it means release from anxiety, healing for loneliness, assurance that life is not lost in any kind of frustration. Because God is our Friend it means release from life's prisons, redemption of suffering, the fellowship of the Church in our conflict with evil." In each chapter the topic and the subtopic stress the need of God, His provision for us, or both these factors.

With a wealth of materials from unexpected sources the interpreter makes his truth luminous to a congregation near Yale University. He bases everything on the kerygma, as a

[2] *In the Secret Place of the Most High* (New York: Charles Scribner's Sons, 1947).

[3] (New York: Harper & Bros., 1954), pp. 9, 91-102.

66

rule indirectly, but never evasively. In a message unusual for a young man—"But If We Suffer with God: Redemption of Suffering" (Rom. 8:16-17)—the main affirmations run as follows. If we suffer with God, we

I. Discover that God suffers with us.
II. Make of our sufferings an offering to God.
III. Enter into a closer fellowship with God.
IV. Come into closer fellowship with God's children.

Sermons by other masters show that pulpit counselors deal with soul disorders of all kinds. A wise man considers only one malady at a time, with only one Bible passage. He does not conduct a free-for-all clinic, or show how many texts of Scripture he knows by heart. He is not a sleight-of-hand showman, but a physician of souls. When Raymond I. Lindquist went back to his pulpit in Hollywood, he preached three morning sermons: "Christ's Solution for the Inferiority Complex" (Exod. 3:11); ". . . for Your Doubt" (John 20:28); ". . . for Human Passion" (John 8:11). Such a man becomes known for the ability to counsel for God in public and in private.

PREACHING ABOUT A BIBLE CASE

The relevant facts about Moses appear in the record about the burning bush (Exod. 3, 4). When he heard God's call to service, this man past middle age uttered five excuses, like such plaints today, but in a different idiom. In any language a duty dodger can say "I." Do not fix attention on his excuses, but on God's way of meeting them with doctrine. In a "Bible study" an expert could deal with all five replies. In a counseling sermon a man does well to consider one. He can let the other four wait for future sermons.

This case presents one of the most useful men in history,

a man almost as big as a mountain. But not until after the Lord takes away that inferiority complex. In the pew yonder sits a man or woman who will become a power for good after some such transforming experience. I could recount such cases, but I prefer to look at this one in the Bible.

PREACHING ABOUT A BIBLE CASE

"Who am I, that I should go?" asks a man potentially strong when he faces a new and dangerous duty. "I will be with thee" (Exod. 3:12a), says the God who never lets a man down. Since the cause has to do with the hearer and the cure relates to God, give each of them a square deal. However much the temptation to intrude, keep out of the picture. Bring these two persons face to face, and keep them there.

A MAN WHO TELLS GOD NO

Be frank with God; tell Him how you feel.
I. A case of a clear call to duty
II. A case of cowardly evasion
III. A case of God's patience
IV. A case of duty done for God

Another case shows how the Lord deals with a young man who holds back from a known duty. At a time when young Jeremiah's world seemed ready to cave in, he heard the voice of God calling him to a difficult duty and perhaps to death. The young man demurred: "Ah, Lord God! behold, I cannot speak: for I am a child." Now comes the text: "I am with thee to deliver thee" (Jer. 1:8b). In the spirit of his coming Redeemer, Jeremiah accepted his hazardous commission and became perhaps the most Christlike man in the Old Testament. Subject here: "The Man Who Tells God Yes."

Among the year's counseling sermons this one about an

inferiority complex may do the most good. Before a nominating committee approaches a man about accepting an important office in church or city, he may need a message about duty, which Wordsworth addresses as "Daughter of the Voice of God!" Later in his "Ode to Duty" the poet comes closer to the spirit of the Bible:

> Love is an unerring light,
> And joy its own security.
> And oft, when in my heart was heard
> Thy timely mandate, I deferred
> The task, in smoother walks to stray;
> But thee I now would serve more strictly, if I may.
>
> . . . .
>
> Give unto me, made lowly wise,
> The spirit of self-sacrifice;
> The confidence of reason give;
> And in the light of truth thy Bondman let me live!

The Bible refers all these matters to God. Take fear, which has become Public Enemy Number Two, with sin itself as Number One. Recently I picked up a concordance and started to count the texts about the wrong sort of fear. Before I got halfway through the list, I grew weary and quit. In the pulpit anyone could take a string of twenty such pearls and make a few comments about each of them. What good would that do the next time a layman gave way to fear? He needs an illuminated text, such as this: "Though I walk through the valley of the shadow of death, I will fear no evil" (Ps. 23:4).

Whatever the text or the subject, the message about fear says much the same thing. Cause—self. Cure—God. Even so, each Bible passage has a different setting and a unique tone color. For example, in the world's noblest description of a storm at sea, deliverance from fear comes to Paul through

69

assurance of Christ's presence, and through concern for the welfare of others. In a counseling sermon a man may not have time to expound this passage or even publicly explain his text. At least he can send the hearer home remembering the fact of Christ's presence in peril, and the need for helping others in distress. The doctrine and the duty!

THE VOICE THAT QUIETS YOUR FEARS

"Fear not, Paul; . . . God hath given thee all them that sail with thee" (Acts 27:24).

In every storm of life the Lord stands by to help.

I. He may permit you to enter into peril.
II. He enables you to conquer every fear.
III. He fills you with concern for persons in distress.

SENSING THE NEEDS OF OTHERS

The pastor ought to apply this principle to his pulpit work. A doctrine about Christ, and a duty to someone in distress. This line of thought may call for a message about "God's Cure of an Honest Doubter." A text stands out in a difficult psalm. Here a strong man of God feels down in the dumps because the righteous suffer while the wicked prosper. The cure comes when he goes to the House of the Lord:

> My flesh and my heart fail;
> But my heart's rock and my portion is God forever.
> (Ps. 73:26 Smith-Goodspeed.)

Two facts stand out here:

I. A good man feels the futility of life.
II. This man finds a foundation in faith.

An expert counselor, John S. Bonnell, advises a minister to end an interview with a word of prayer and a written prescription from the Bible. One text, and that not long! The same principle applies to pulpit counseling. If chosen with care and handled with skill, a text may do a disconsolate soul more good than anything else in the hour of worship. In such a long and rich text as Matt. 11:28-30 the counselor can single out the one part that he wishes to stress. Here again, note the doctrine and the duty, which ought to become a delight.

CHRIST'S GIFT OF RESTFULNESS

"I will give you rest, . . . rest unto your souls" (Matt. 11:28-30).
  I. Restfulness through worship: "Come unto me."
  II. Restfulness through work: "Take my yoke."
  III. Restfulness through waiting: "Learn of me."

One note may seem to be sadly lacking so far. Restfulness comes through getting right with God. In a sermon from this text about "Rest," Brooks says near the end:

The great burden and weariness of life, when any man becomes conscious of it, is sin. "I could bear anything if I had not done wrong," the true man says. Then begins the turmoil of self-reproach and self-contempt . . . which beats and drives the poor, bewildered soul about as the sea beats the wrecked ship, abandoned to its power. . . . It is almost a mockery to talk of everything else Christ can do for a man, until we tell first what He can do for a man's sins.[4]

A pastor ought also to preach on doubt. Henry van Dyke wrote an able book about *The Gospel for an Age of Doubt.* Today a pulpit counselor thinks more about the way the Lord deals with one honest doubter. Doubt means intellectual uncertainty about a major truth of Christianity. Doubt does not mean being bothered about tiddlywinks. In one of his chap-

[4] *The Law of Growth* (New York: E. P. Dutton & Co., 1910), p. 146.

ters van Dyke shows how to deal with a young doubter. Introduce him to Christ.

The Gospel of Christ is the gospel of a person who saves men from sin. And herein it comes very close to the heart of a doubting age. . . . This is the essence of Christianity, the only gospel that is worth preaching in all ways to all men, that Jesus Christ is God who loves us in order that we may learn to love one another.[5]

Such preaching rests on doctrine about Christ as the Revealer of God. For a case turn to young Thomas, constitutionally a doubter. In the Fourth Gospel he appears three times, and each time he voices a doubt (11:16; 14:5; 20:25). After the Resurrection of Christ this young "senior in the seminary" still has honest doubts. Instead of reproaching him bitterly, the risen Lord takes him in hand, offers the evidence he demands, and leads him into radiant belief.

GOOD NEWS FOR A YOUNG DOUBTER

"Except I shall see . . . , I will not believe" (John 20:25b).
Christ loves this young man, frank, eager, wistful.
    I. Our Lord deals kindly with an honest doubter.
        Shows sympathy for this friend who suffers.
        Encourages him to deal with the matter squarely.
        Looks on his doubt as a disorder in the soul.
        Encourages him to look for relief right now.
    II. Our Lord stands ready to remove your doubts.
        Wishes you to bring your doubts to Him, frankly.
        Offers you all the evidence you need.
        Stands ready to change you into a believer.
        Expects you to help other doubters.

The doubt may concern the Bible. Van Dyke used to say that a typical congregation sang best of all the old-time hymn

---

[5] (New York: The Macmillan Co., 1896), pp. 75, 315.

> How firm a foundation, ye saints of the Lord,
> Is laid for your faith in His excellent Word!

But what if a young man's doubt has to do with the written Word? Guidance here may come to the minister through a book by A. C. Craig, *Preaching in a Scientific Age.*[6] He says that for the young man's grandfather "the Bible was a book of answers to life's problems, authoritative and inspired. For the young man it has become a book of problems, to many of which there seem to be no authoritative answers." Many young people today "are like Polar explorers who waken up one morning to discover that their camp, instead of being pitched on the mainland, is adrift on an ice-floe."

My heart goes out to this young friend. Like most men in the ministry, I went through such a period. I do not wonder now that young people accept what they have been taught in college and have read in books. Still I know that the cure for honest doubt comes through getting the young friend to become well acquainted with the living Christ. Instead of urging him to believe in Christ because of this truth or that, a wise interpreter brings his friend face to face with Christ Himself and trusts the Lord to do His own clarifying. Again and again in my preaching to doubters I have seen Him do this very thing. In this kind of pulpit counseling almost everything depends on a minister's knowledge of doctrine as it centers in the living Christ.

QUALIFYING AS A PULPIT COUNSELOR

Even the ablest young pastor must learn how to do pulpit counseling. He should understand the heart needs of men and know the resources of Christian doctrine. Then he must

---

[6] (New York: Charles Scribner's Sons, 1954), pp. 24-25.

know how to employ these insights. He ought to decide which sort of counseling sermons he wishes to preach. Does he plan to base everything on the grace of God and to bid the seeker trust only in Him? Or does the interpreter plan to rely on up-to-date psychology as a substitute for Christian doctrine? This latter course has become known as the "cult of reassurance."

At Princeton Seminary an able graduate student analyzed the sermons of a preacher second to none in popular effectiveness. The student discovered that this man appealed mainly to what William McDougall used to call "the instinct of self-assertion." In much the same way a man known to me only through his books has a volume of interesting sermons under the title *The Importance of Being Ourselves*. One sermon bears the heading "Only Man Is Sacred." In a sense all of that holds true; but if I were a doubter, groping after God, this emphasis on the human side of things would bewilder me. Many a man who comes to church knows that he is not the best fellow in the world, and that he cannot live up to his ideal self.

Herein lies one of the chief perils of the ministry today. In every congregation, says Charles R. Brown, there is at least one thief who needs to hear about the mercy of God. To him the pulpit counselor ought somehow to say: "Down on your knees, sir, and confess your sins. Resolve to make restitution, and receive the forgiveness of your sins." In much of the sermonic literature in recent years, this gospel note has often seemed to be muted, if not missing. As for the remedy, that calls for a Christian doctrine in every counseling sermon.

A nondoctrinal sermon may affect a man like a shot in the arm. A minister with a dynamic personality can make a hearer feel ready to attempt the impossible. The effect may last for a week, and then he needs another shot in the arm. In Philadelphia, according to a biographer, whenever S. Weir Mitchell came into a sickroom, "a highly charged electric current started through the dormant mental and physical being." If Mitchell had become a pulpit counselor of the reassuring sort, he could have electrified his hearers every Sunday, and sent them away to praise his mesmeric powers.

A change for the better has more than begun. Ever since World War II, if not before, ministers have been wanting to get away from horizontal preaching, where everything seems to depend on the charm of the speaker and the resources of the hearer. More than a few pastors have found that by preaching doctrine, often indirectly, they can lead men to look up, and not to think first about "the importance of being themselves." In the preaching of doctrine for the relief of soul disorders, a physician of souls needs more than an electrifying personality and a winning voice (Ezek. 33:30-33). He needs to know God, and to have a personal experience of transforming grace, as fresh as the morning dew.

CHAPTER SIX

THE DOCTRINE
IN ETHICAL SERMONS

WE NOW COME TO THE MOST DIFFICULT MATTER SO far. What should a pastor do about ethical problems as they relate to his community? In the pulpit should he attack them head on, act as an artful dodger, or preach about them indirectly? A man with a martyr complex may try to reform the world all at once. A coward keeps quiet about controversial issues. A wise man follows the biblical custom of dealing with moral problems on the basis of doctrine. In First Corinthians, for example, Paul did not dodge any moral issue that concerned believers there. Some problems he dealt with directly; others, indirectly; all of them he considered in the light of Christian love and the life everlasting.

FACING MORAL ISSUES SQUARELY

Before a man decides such a matter, he ought to consider the needs of the home church and community. During the period before Easter he has welcomed many new members. What do they need from the pulpit? Clear, interesting sermons about what to believe, how to live, and what to hope for. As for ethics they need to know the Christian attitude toward liquor and vice, marriage and divorce, money and its use, forgiveness of wrongs and how to treat members of another race.

About such matters new converts feel confused. So do church members of long standing. The pastor may share the bewilderment. He may have been puzzled by the late Fred M. Vinson, Chief Justice of the United States Supreme Court, who rendered this decision: "Nothing is more certain in modern society than the principle that there are no absolutes; that . . . a standard has meaning only when associated with the considerations which gave birth to the nomenclature. . . . All concepts are relative."[1] Whew!

Where does that leave a man who must decide between right and wrong? Ought he to obey any of the Ten Words or revere the Sermon on the Mount? He knows about standard time, standard weights and measures, standards for purity of food and drugs. Are there no moral standards for a man who wears a garment warranted not to shrink in the rain? The idea of relativity in morals has infected people in the Church as well as out in town. They need to learn that according to Christ some acts are right, always and everywhere, and other acts are wrong, dastardly wrong.

The Bible teaches that duty rests on doctrine. According to Oscar Cullmann, master theologian of Switzerland, "in primitive Christianity ethics without theology is absolutely inconceivable." [2] He might also have said that in the New Testament, doctrine divorced from duty seems rare. Dorothy L. Sayers, the lay interpreter, agrees about the doctrinal basis of Christian duty: "It is worse than useless for Christians to talk about the importance of Christian morality unless they are prepared to take their stand upon the fundamentals of Christian theology."[3] The converse holds true: It is scarcely Christian to teach a doctrine without reference to a corresponding duty.

In any one year the preaching of doctrine ought to bulk

[1] Quoted by Edwin M. Poteat, *Mandate to Humanity* (New York and Nashville: Abingdon Press, 1953), p. 14n.
[2] *Christ and Time*, tr. F. V. Filson (Philadelphia: Westminster Press, 1950), p. 224.
[3] *Op. cit.*, p. 28.

larger than the preaching of duty. If people know and believe Bible truth about God and man, they can solve many moral problems. If they do not know such doctrines, they have no mighty reason for doing their duty. Still the interpreter ought to stress what his Bible passage stresses. Karl Barth seems to act strangely here. In writing ably about First Corinthians, a book full of ethics, Barth practically ignores duty and stresses a doctrine, *The Resurrection of the Dead* (1933).

The Scriptures often present duty in "life situations." In Exodus a man of God faces an overlord and demands freedom for an enslaved people. The speaker puts everything on a religious basis: "Thus saith the Lord God of Israel, Let my people go." The overlord refuses: "I know not the Lord, neither will I let Israel go" (5:1c, 2b). A dramatic contrast between a man who does right and one who does wrong. An opening for a "life-situation sermon": "How to Choose Between Right and Wrong."

    I. A man who does a difficult duty because he believes in God
   II. A man who refuses to do right because he does not believe in God

A similar contrast appears between Paul and Felix (Acts 24:25): Paul spoke out, boldly; Felix trembled, abjectly. The one believed in God; the other did not. Also between Christ and Cain: Christ died for His enemies; Cain killed his brother (I John 3:12). Today every person is "stamped with the family likeness of Cain or of Christ." Would that every son of Cain might accept Christ! Meanwhile, you might as well plead with a tiger to sheathe his claws as to suggest that Cain "mend his manners." He needs Christ.[4]

---

[4] See a striking sermon by Robert Law in *The Grand Adventure* (London: Hodder & Stoughton, Ltd., 1916), "Cain and Christ," pp. 185-95.

PUTTING THE GOOD BEFORE THE BAD

The Bible usually puts Christ before Cain; we often reverse the order. Without making a careful count, I estimate that in three cases out of four the Bible puts the good before the bad. This may not hold true in isolated verses, but the Bible was not written in isolated verses. A man has a right to change the Bible order; but if he does so, his sermon may seem anticlimactic. The average hearer thinks more about the bad than about the good. If the latter part of the message deals with the bad, by contrast, that goes far to insure a climax. Many a modern sermon starts with a wealth of human interest and oozes out near the end.

The important fact is that in the Bible a duty always grows out of a doctrine. Even in Proverbs and in James the sacred writers base morality on theology. So do the Ten Commandments: "I am the Lord thy God, which have brought thee out of . . . the house of bondage" (Exod. 20:2). Duty based on redemption! God has a special claim on everyone whom He delivers from bondage. The principle of basing duty on doctrine appears in a difficult Bible book, Leviticus, which stresses holiness. The most important chapter ethically starts this way: "Ye shall be holy: for I the Lord your God am holy" (19:2b). Then the chapter stresses the unholiness—lack of likeness to God—in stealing, lying, and committing perjury; in hatred, vengeance, and holding a grudge.

Holiness means likeness to God, resulting in love for a neighbor. "Thou shalt love thy neighbor as thyself" (19:18). Our Lord uses these words to show the meaning of a man's religion; but before He says anything about love for a neighbor, he stresses love for God. Christian ethics: God first; neighbor second; self last (Luke 10:27). Doctrine, duty, discipleship! To the hearer—interest, more interest, most interest. What a climactic order, and all about love!

Loving God first stands out, also, in Deuteronomy. In this book dear to the heart of Christ the keynote "thy God" rings out more than three hundred times. "Religion in Terms of Loyalty," which means love in action. The most important passage deals with "Religious Nurture in the Home" (6:4-9). Here too God stands out first, and love prevails. As head of the household the father ought to lead in making a home like heaven. By talk at the table, by pictures on the walls, by other ways of appealing to "eye-gate," and by living in the spirit of love, he and his wife should lead their little ones to put God first. This is not only first-class homiletics; it is the heart of biblical religion.

LEARNING FROM THE NEW TESTAMENT

So we might go through the Bible, everywhere finding that doctrine determines duty. In the Sermon on the Mount the truth of the Kingdom leads to ethics, as well as eschatology. In dealing with any Bible passage, here or elsewhere, if the dominant verb is imperative, a man looks for something about duty. When our Lord says, "Let your light so shine" (Matt. 5:16), he refers to good works, though not to earn salvation.

Again our Lord says: "Suffer the little children to come unto me" (Mark 10:14). The context shows that duty toward children grows out of doctrine about the Kingdom. The same holds true of teachings about marriage and divorce. In the pulpit, as in counseling, a man ought not to discuss either subject without bringing little children into the picture. If none have come to bless a home, that may be partly why a marriage is headed for the rocks. All this teaching relates to doctrine about God as our Father.

In these matters we often turn to Paul. Sometimes we treat him unfairly. When he wrote to Corinth about problems local and temporary, we interpret his teachings as hard-and-fast laws binding on us today. In Ephesians, a "circular letter," he considered no local tangles. Here he showed himself a believer in marriage. "Husbands, love your wives, even as Christ also loved the church, and gave himself for it" (Eph. 5:25). Then follows one of the noblest panegyrics ever uttered about the Church as the Bride of Christ. What would this mean if the writer did not cherish a lofty ideal of marriage and home as earth's nearest approach to heaven?

A Unitarian scholar refers to Wesleyan theology as centering in the home. In the "transfiguration of the family" God is Father, and man is His child.

Repentance . . . is but the homesickness of the soul, and the uninterrupted and watchful care of the parent is the fairest earthly type of the unfailing forgiveness of God. . . . The family . . . is not designed to make life easier, but to make life better. . . . It has its troubles, and they draw hearts together. It has its joys, and they are multiplied by being shared. . . . The pure love which creates a stable family still sanctifies multitudes of such homes, set far back from the stormy agitations of the time.[5]

This principle about ethics applies to the use of money. The Bible says much on the subject, not least in the teachings of Christ. He and the apostles base such teachings on doctrine. Sometimes because of God's sovereignty, again because of Christ's death, the New Testament tells us what to do with money. Sometimes the teaching is indirect. In I Cor. 15 Paul has fifty-eight verses about the Resurrection and two following verses about "the collection for the saints" (16:1-2). In II Cor.

[5] Francis G. Peabody, *Jesus Christ and the Social Question* (New York: The Macmillan Co., 1900), pp. 147, 174, 181-82.

8 and 9 he gives detailed instructions about money and says only a little about the motive: "Ye know the grace of our Lord Jesus Christ, that, though he was rich, yet for your sakes he became poor, that ye through his poverty might be rich" (8:9). "How rich He was—How poor He became—How rich He made us!"

A wise preacher follows much the same principle of securing variety. In a doctrinal message he pays some attention to the resulting duty. In an ethical sermon he points out the underlying doctrine. As a rule he does not stress both doctrine and duty equally. Such a double-barreled discourse would delight seasoned sermontasters, but it would confuse a new convert who needs practical guidance. Even if a minister could deal with two large subjects in one sermon, a hearer might not be able to digest a double meal. A good deal of the prevailing doctrinal and ethical ignorance among churchgoers may be due to our habit of setting too much food on the table. An occasional layman can cope with a six-course banquet, if prepared by a culinary artist; but a new convert thrives better on a simpler diet.

In preparing a sermon, present what the passage stresses. In almost every preaching part of Holy Writ, either a doctrine or a duty predominates. If the man in the pulpit has an "exegetical conscience," he stresses doctrine where his passage teaches doctrine, and duty where his passage teaches duty. If he tried to reach two major objectives in a single sermon, he might misrepresent the Bible and bewilder the hearer.

DEALING WITH DELICATE ISSUES

By preaching indirectly a minister can deal with a delicate issue, such as race or war. In the New Testament interracial brotherhood looms large. For example, think about Peter's change of attitude toward non-Jews. In a single hour on a housetop he changed his practical philosophy of life because of a vision that still shines out from "the most exciting book in the New Testament." "What God hath cleansed, that call not thou common" (Acts 10:15b). "I see quite plainly that God has no favourites" (vs. 34a Moffatt). Peter showed his new spirit by welcoming non-Jews to his home overnight (vs. 23a), and by going to be a guest in a non-Jewish house (vs. 48). The walls of racial separation have fallen down. Why? Because Peter has learned a new lesson about what it means to be a Christian.

Starting with one of these texts, a minister can show what the Bible here means in terms of today. Without reference to local conditions he can give the lay hearer enough light to guide him in making his own application. The sermon may issue from Acts 10:34b: "God is no respecter of persons." The Greek means that "God shows no partiality" (Goodspeed); more simply, He has no pets.

    I. God has no pets among the people He has made.
      Once He chose the Hebrews; He has chosen us.
      He wished the Hebrews to love other races.
      He has always loved men of every race.
   II. God wishes us to become like our Father.
      Every man should be loyal to his race.
      He should be ready for human brotherhood.
      The guidance comes from the Holy Spirit.

In private conference a layman may ask: "What should I do about my new Negro neighbors?" In the South, where I lived for years, I do not know the answer. I should assure the inquirer of two things: God knows; He will guide you in doing His will. Then I should add a third: As for me and my family, we treat members of every race as brothers and sisters, on the street, in church, and at our home. "If any man's will is to do his will [God's], he shall know." (John 7:17a R.S.V.) "The Illumination of Obedience!"

As with questions about taking part in war, the matter of race is more complex than preachers make it seem. No minister can answer all these questions, glibly or overnight. Meanwhile he can thank God for any improved relations between white folk and Negroes, and pray for the time when there will be in Protestant churches no segregation on Sunday or any other day. He can also rejoice in these words from the autobiography of Robert R. Moton, the late principal of Tuskegee Institute. After a firsthand study of living conditions among working people in Europe he wrote: "Whatever may be the disadvantages and inconveniences of my race in America, I would rather be a Negro in the United States than anybody else in any country in the world." [6]

This forward-looking leader was thinking about hope. He knew that in our land any member of his race could hope for better things in the lives of his children. This hope comes from the Bible, especially the book of Exodus, the source of the noblest spirituals, such as "Let my people go." Centuries after the Exodus, Paul wrote as a descendant of enslaved people: "[God has] made from one every nation of men to live on all the face of the earth" (Acts 17:26a R.S.V.). "There is neither Jew nor Greek, there is neither bond nor free, there is neither male nor female: for ye are all one in Christ Jesus" (Gal. 3:28). One in opportunity, which means hope.

The Bible teaching about race is clear. The minister should live in its light and preach it to others. How? The tendency is to talk about the race problem. If I were a Negro, I should not wish anyone to refer to me or my wife, my child or my

[6] *Finding a Way Out* (New York: Page & Co., 1922), p. 152.

race, as a problem. Neither should I wish anyone to discuss the matter belligerently. "Let all men know your forbearance" (Phil. 4:5a R.S.V.), which means "sweet reasonableness." Here I have learned much from a "candid, behind-the-scenes story of a trial judge," a Hebrew in New York City. *Mutatis mutandis*, what he says ought to hold true of every minister who preaches ethics. I give a paraphrase:

The trial judge needs to be honest, industrious, and courageous. He ought also to be a gentleman. If he knows something about the law, that helps. If he does not yet know all he should, he can set up an evening law school at home. Once Bernard Botein presided at a trial with opposing attorneys whom he calls "Brawl" and "Bellows," who fought tooth and nail. The judge halted the proceedings and addressed the jury. He apologized for the lawyers, who had ignored the claims of justice and decency. Then he ordered them to proceed with the case, on its merits, and to act as gentlemen.[7]

A preacher's work differs from that of a lawyer or a judge. Still the "intimate record" suggests a few reflections. Before any man discusses a matter of right and wrong, he should know his facts. In the seminary, and more fully, in the pastor's study, he should have mastered the kerygma before he interprets the didache. On the other hand, as the present Chief Justice of the United States Supreme Court has shown, a man can learn the law more perfectly after he becomes a judge. So can the minister learn the doctrine on which he bases the teaching of a duty. The best way to become a preacher of Bible ethics is to keep doing this difficult kind of pulpit work, often indirectly. If so, whenever you enter the pulpit, do not lay down the law, but hold up a light.

[7] See Bernard Botein, *Trial Judge* (New York: Simon & Schuster, Inc., 1952), pp. 3, 36.

CHAPTER SEVEN

THE PREACHING
OF DOCTRINE DIRECTLY

W E HAVE BEEN THINKING ABOUT DOCTRINAL PREACHING
as indirect. After six or eight years of such pulpit work
a man may discover that even the most attentive churchgoers
know next to nothing about Christian doctrine. In fact, he
may need to clarify his own thinking. While I believe in
preaching doctrine indirectly, I feel that the time has come
for doing more of it straight from the shoulder. By preaching
doctrine directly I mean that the text and the topic, the
introduction and the conclusion, the main headings and everything else, point the listener to a certain doctrine, as clear as
crystal. I consider the preparation of such a sermon the
most difficult task a preacher undertakes, except when he has
a doctrinal series.

UNDERSTANDING A DOCTRINE

The difficulty may spring from not understanding a doctrine
well enough to explain it. A Frenchman once said something like this: "I know God fairly well; but when I try to
tell someone else, I find I do not know Him." Any of us
might preach an inspiring message about God as Light or Life.
How many of us know what we mean by Light or Life? Sometimes a man wonders if he understands anything. Even Isaac
Newton, first among scientists, late in life referred to himself
as a boy playing on the seashore and finding a prettier shell
than usual, while the ocean of truth lay before him undis-

covered. So a man's hesitation about preaching a doctrine directly may spring from humility.

Fortunately, this kind of pulpit work does not call for "superficial omniscience." No sermon ought to divest a doctrine of its mystery. If the mystery of our holy faith were removed, nothing worth having would remain. No one can explain how God performs a miracle or brings about a new birth. If anyone could account for such an experience, his explanation would seem miraculous. On the other hand, a man with no powers approaching genius can learn what some part of the Bible says about a certain aspect of revealed truth, and what difference it ought to make in the life of a layman. If any person attempted to do more, he might seem like the fabled Atlas who bore on his shoulders the weight of the world. In order to preach well, a man needs to let his spirit soar; and then the truth will seem to sing.

> I know not how that Bethlehem's Babe
> Could in the Godhead be;
> I only know the manger Child
> Has brought God's life to me.[1]

A man who tries to explain the Virgin Birth undertakes to carry a needless load. He resembles an Irish woman on her way to market, carrying a large basket full of potatoes for sale. When a passing driver invites her to sit in the back part of his cart, she insists on standing up and carrying her load. As for the moral, van Dyke used to say: "Never tell a tale without a moral, and never tag the moral to a tale." For example, take the doctrine justification by faith. In preaching about it, why make a detour and discuss a related question: "How is it

---

[1] Harry W. Farrington.

possible for God to forgive sins?" Once an assistant came to R. W. Dale and asked him this question. As the author of a scholarly book on *The Atonement*, Dale replied:

Give up troubling, my friend, about how it was possible for God to forgive sin. Go straight and tell the people that God does forgive sin. Tell them straight that Christ died for their sins. It is the fact that the people want most to know, and not your theory or mine about how it was or is possible.[2]

When a man preaches a doctrine directly, he makes no detours. John A. Broadus, prince of scholars, has a sermon about Justification by Faith (Rom. 5:1). The first main part shows the meaning of justification: "Paul's Greek word does not mean to *make* just, but to *regard* as just. . . . How would God treat you, if you were a righteous man? . . . He would smile on you [as He does now in the face of Jesus Christ]. That is what Paul means by justification. And when Martin Luther found that out he found peace."

The second part takes up faith. "A man might say, if God proposes to deal with those who are not just, as if they were, why does he condition it upon their believing the Gospel of Jesus Christ?" The answer, briefly, is that through our believing in Christ the heavenly Father intends to make us just and holy.

The last main part has to do with God's gift of peace. Peace here and now, not on the basis of a man's attainments, but because of his faith in Christ. "We cannot have peace with God as long as we cling to the notion that we are going to deserve it. . . . If we believe in the Lord Jesus Christ, our *justification* is perfect. We can never be more justified than

[2] A. W. W. Dale (a son), *The Life of R. W. Dale of Birmingham* (New York: Dodd, Mead & Co., 1899), p. 643.

88

we are now justified. . . . Let us have peace with God, though we have perpetual conflict with sin." [3]

Any sermon worthy of its high calling raises questions. If vital, they call for other messages. In the volume by Broadus the next sermon takes up the question "How the Gospel Makes Men Holy" (Rom. 7:24-25, about the warfare in a man's soul). The sermon following: "Intense Concern for the Salvation of Others" (Rom. 9:3, about willingness to be accursed for the sake of unsaved people). So it seems that a sermon directly doctrinal singles out one important truth and then deals with nothing else. Herein lies much of our difficulty, due to our habit of discursiveness.

RELATING A DOCTRINE TO LIFE

If a minister understands what some part of the Bible teaches about a doctrine, he faces the difficulty of relating it to the interests and needs of the hearers. He may know what justification meant to Paul and to Luther, to Ritschl and to Broadus. Does the local interpreter know what difference this truth ought to make in the everyday living of Sam Small and his wife, and their teen-age sons? What has one of them in common with giants and saints of other days? At least this much: a gap, if not a chasm, between attainments and ideals.

> And ah for a man to arise in me,
> That the man I am may cease to be!

Many a churchgoer in quest of a better life has explored more than one blind alley. Why should he have to hear another sermon about theology?

Get the hearer to see that being good comes through faith

[3] *Sermons and Addresses* (New York: George H. Doran Co., 1896), "Let Us Have Peace with God," pp. 85-96.

in God. That the person who has lost his way or never has found it can enter into peace through faith in Christ. No one sermon can answer all a seeker's questions, but any such message ought to show him how to get started on the upward way. Bunyan once did so: "Do you see yonder wicket-gate?" "No." "Do you see yonder shining light?" "I think I do." "Keep that light in your eye, and go up directly thereto, so shalt thou see the gate; at which, when thou knockest, it shall be told thee what thou shalt do."

Some other time preach about salvation by grace. Among people with a Roman Catholic background Luther rightly stressed justification by faith. This teaching came from Paul, but the Apostle looked beyond faith to grace: "By grace you have been saved through faith; and this is not your own doing, it is the gift of God" (Eph. 2:8 R.S.V.). To get the "feel" of this high truth, read the biography of Jowett, whose favorite word was "grace." He seldom preached directly about the doctrine, but his life and work showed much about the elusive word "grace."

You cannot define it, but then you cannot define anything that is really lovely. Still less can you define Love itself. . . . There is no word I have wrestled so much with as Grace. . . . If anyone is in love he does not need to take down a dictionary to find out its meaning. . . . Grace is divine favor, but it means much more than this. It is holy love radiating from the soul of the Eternal into the souls of His children, and transforming them into His likeness for His service.[4]

With a young friend in the pew this teaching about grace may go against the grain. In school he has learned from Emerson about "Self-Reliance" and from W. E. Henley:

[4] Arthur Porritt, *John Henry Jowett* (New York: George H. Doran Co., 1924), pp. 17-18.

> I am the master of my fate;
> I am the captain of my soul.

In church the young man may wonder why the pastor chooses an old-time hymn, such as the following by Charles Wesley:

> Plenteous grace with Thee is found,
> Grace to cover all my sin.

If the minister devotes an entire sermon to some aspect of grace, the young man may wonder what this has to do with the next day's work or with his plans for life. Herein lies no small part of the difficulty in preaching a doctrine directly. Unless one knows how to do it superbly, it may seem otherworldly, irrelevant, and outmoded, as much so as Edmund Spenser's exquisite poem, "The Fairie Queen."

And yet this fact of God's grace lies at the heart of all religion and all life. Paul and Augustine, Luther and John Wesley, with a host of others, had to wait beyond youth to discover that a man cannot save himself. Instead of passing by a parade of such witnesses, a minister does well to study one at a time. Better still, like Thomas Chalmers at a rural church in Kilmany, a pastor may find that he needs to make this discovery himself. Always thereafter, except when he has an occasional bout with Giant Despair, the minister will rejoice in the soul's discovery of grace as the most glorious fact about God. He will also find that acceptance of grace sets a man free for larger and more joyous service.

PRESENTING A TRUTH ATTRACTIVELY

Transforming effects follow preaching about grace, but only if a minister can do it well. Unintentionally, he may let God seem ungracious. By sitting at the feet of Paul anyone can learn how to make this truth a fact of daily experience.

The doctrine reaches down to bedrock deeper by far than any man's experience can go; but every interpreter needs to have such an experience, repeated every day, and to enjoy fellowship with others who rely on grace.

This truth shines out everywhere in the works of John Bunyan. In *Pilgrim's Progress* he shows the meaning and the glory of faith. In a spiritual autobiography, *Grace Abounding to the Chief of Sinners*, this poetic preacher of doctrine makes clear the meaning and the glory of a truth about grace, truth that sounds forth in *Pilgrim's Progress*. Christian cries out in distress: "I sink in deep waters; the billows go over my head; all his waves go over me." Then Hopeful responds: "Be of good cheer, my brother. I feel the bottom, and it is good."

> How firm a foundation, ye saints of the Lord,
> Is laid for your faith in His excellent Word!

That foundation is God's grace.

FINDING TIME TO PREPARE

The main difficulty about such pulpit works lies in a different realm. Many a pastor holds back from preaching doctrine directly, not because of these other obstacles, but because he has not time to do all the basic reading and other spadework. Year after year the daily schedule of the pastor gets more complicated. Still it bears some resemblance to a word picture from yesterday. Even in olden days more than one pastor felt "committeed to death":

While the preacher should live the life of his community he must not allow himself to be distracted by a multitude of engagements and to be cumbered by much serving. The passion for committees and the lust for meetings seem to be American weaknesses. I have known pastors who were always so busy rushing about to keep appointments of this sort that they could no longer look long enough in one direction to see God's face anywhere.[5]

As for the remedy, that would require another book, which I have tried to write.[6] I feel untold sympathy for a minister in charge of a merry-go-round that he must keep moving until he suffers a nervous breakdown or else leaves for another field of labor equally exacting. Here I offer two suggestions, the better one first. (1) Get lay friends to represent you and the congregation on community and interchurch committees. Almost every local church has gifted men and women, retired or semiretired, eager for service that calls for brains and imagination. When they learn that their minister needs time for study in the spirit of prayer, they rally to his support, but only if he opens the door. Such lay leaders are already at work, with tasks equal to their powers, in congregations large and small. Strange as the fact may seem, many a person ready for service finds more of an opportunity in a large church than in a small one, where the pastor tries to do everything himself and gets lost in a maze.

(2) If you cannot organize a twenty-four-hour day so as to leave a morning largely free for study in the spirit of prayer, do not attempt to preach much doctrine directly. Nobody can prepare this kind of pulpit food if he has to rely on shreds and patches of time and material. Who wants pulpit doctrine half-baked or half-burned? But be sure that you are doing only such other tasks as the Lord has assigned to you personally. Moses had to learn this lesson (Exod. 18:13-26). From an older man he heard about what we call "division of labor," so that God's leader does not break down or develop stomach

[5] Pepper, op. cit., p. 93.
[6] *Pastoral Leadership* (New York and Nashville: Abingdon Press, 1949).

ulcers. From the Holy Spirit the apostles also learned to dele-
gate necessary work, so that they could give themselves to
"prayer, and to the ministry of the word" (Acts 6:4). The
Lord does not commission and train a man to preach and then
put him in charge of a three-ring circus, taken over from a
predecessor, and destined to keep growing "bigger and better"
under a person too busy to study and too bothered to pray.
Son of Martha, "thou art careful and troubled about many
things: but one thing is needful" (Luke 10:41).

Another difficulty may not seem formidable, but it calls for
notice. The hour of worship may not allow time enough for
preaching a doctrine directly. Some of us have been "enriching the service," and none too soon; but we have had to curtail
the sermon. If boys and girls come to worship God and remain
for the benediction, sixty minutes may prove long enough,
and that without haste or omission of anything vital. Unless
a man can reserve at least twenty-two minutes for a sermon,
how can he preach directly about such a doctrine as salvation
by grace?

If the day's program calls for two separate hours of public
worship, there need be no such difficulty. At eleven the hour
of worship may include an inspiring message used of God in
helping the young in heart to form a lifelong habit of attend-
ing and enjoying church, with a good deal of stress on the
sermon. A second service may come at eight-thirty, four, eight,
or some other hour that ought not to be shifted. In a community where the Roman Catholic church nearby holds
services from before daybreak until high noon, Protestants
need more than one opportunity for public worship. Two
different services can meet two different sorts of needs and
appeal to different kinds of people. As for preparation, many
of us, when in practice, have found it as easy to prepare two

sermons as when we have had only one. We have also found it easier to preach at the second service than at the first.

You can count on a "carry" and interest on a Sunday evening, that you cannot command at a more formal service. There is a natural "unbending" both on your part and the people's. Use that helpful atmosphere wisely. In dealing with a doctrine, don't dissect it as if it were a corpse, some dead thing outside yourself which you regard only with intellectual curiosity, but use it as "the body of our faith" by which we live. . . . Translate theology into religion and the abstract into the concrete. Avoid especially played out phrases and old shibboleths, once good coin to those who minted them, but now out of common currency.[7]

James Black assumes that the second service calls for a sermon more or less doctrinal. I am pleading that often it be directly so. I believe that every community needs at least one church open at night, with an opportunity for people to learn what they can hear only in a teaching church. If local conditions do not favor having open house Sunday night all through the year, any official board will allow the minister to have special services at strategic seasons, such as during Advent, Lent, and through Holy Week. In each case the occasion would call for a doctrinal sermon, not longer than thirty minutes.

A pastor on a circuit may insist that he does well if he gets to Cream Ridge, or some other charge, once on Sunday. In that case he can plan by the month, so that the sheep will not graze too long in the same pasture. According to the season he can arrange for a month of inspiring messages and another month of teaching sermons. Such a program would help to avoid what seems to mark most circuit preaching. It gets to be known as "deadly dull."

[7] James Black, *The Mystery of Preaching* (Westwood, N. J.: Fleming H. Revell Co., 1924), pp. 151-52. Used by permission of the publisher.

Whatever the program, make every doctrinal message more interesting than anything else in town. In New York City a pastor was asked to intercede for the opening of a neighboring night club whose doors had been padlocked. He could not comply, but he returned the compliment by asking for a motto that had adorned the walls of the night club. If I had the means, I should like to give every young minister an illuminated replica of this motto to hang over the desk in his study:[8]

| NEVER A DULL LULL |

---

[8] I am here indebted to John Ellis Large of New York City.

CHAPTER EIGHT

THE CALL FOR
A DOCTRINAL SERIES

ACCORDING TO THE SEASON A MINISTER WISHES TO preach a number of consecutive sermons about the Incarnation, the Atonement, the Resurrection, or the Holy Spirit. Every thoughtful preacher has a degree of continuity from week to week, if only to encourage him in serious reading, according to a self-made plan. Also, laymen need to watch the Christian drama unfold from stage to stage. Still a man may hesitate to announce a series. If he finds it hard to prepare a single doctrinal sermon, how can he cope with a series? The longer the series, the larger the difficulty.

When a novice preaches a series of five sermons, he may find that the fourth one falters and the fifth fails. Perhaps he does not have a series, carefully unified and climactic, but five sermons where he ought to have three. In a series, as in a continued story, if the hearer's interest does not keep rising week after week, the sermonizer may have lost his pains. These obstacles may seem insurmountable, but not to a man of faith. "Who art thou, O great mountain? before Zerubbabel thou shalt become a plain; and he shall bring forth the top stone with shoutings of Grace, grace" (Zech. 4:7 A.S.V.).

Let the shoutings come in the study after the last of the series. They will come if the master builder has prepared a "top stone," so that the successive sermons lead up to a single unified impression, visible to the eye of every beholder. For such reasons James M. Barrie often planned first the closing act of a drama. The maker of a series forms the habit of having the whole in sight and the materials well in hand before he starts work on the first sermon, or makes any announcement of the series.

Brooks knew about these difficulties. Still he recommended a "prolonged and connected course of sermons [as] a safeguard against mere flightiness and partialness in the choice of topics." He also sounded a warning: "Where the serpent grows too long it is difficult to have the vitality distributed through all his length. . . . Too many courses of sermons start with a very vital head, that draws behind it by and by a very lifeless tail." [1] In full view of the difficulties let us consider a series on the first main part of the Apostles' Creed. Later we shall consider serial preaching by a man who does not subscribe to a creed.

PREACHING ABOUT THE CREED

When I was young, I prepared a series with eight sermons. In a church bulletin or on a printed card I would begin each line with the date and at the end omit the text. In first-class printing, or mimeographing, white space helps to make a big thing seem big. As for little things, leave them out; but be sure about the spelling. Every series needs a general title. In both title and topics the stress ought to fall on doctrine.

The Creed in Christian Thinking
Practical Sermons About the Apostles' Creed

The Importance of a Living Creed—I Pet. 3:15
The Goodness of God Our Father—Matt. 6:9
The Centrality of Jesus Christ—Col. 1:18b
The Supremacy of the Cross—I Cor. 15:3
The Power of Christ's Resurrection—Phil. 3:10ab
The Blessedness of the Ascension—Acts 1:9

---

[1] *Op. cit.*, pp. 154-55. Used by permission of Zondervan Publishing House.

The Promise of the Final Return—Acts 1:11
The Fact of the Judgment Day—II Cor. 5:10

Two omissions call for comment. (1) "The Wonders of God's Creative Work" (Gen. 1:1). In a day when young people study more about science than anything else, they need to see God as the Maker of everything but evil. (2) "The Mystery of the Virgin Birth" (Luke 1:35). According to my most learned teacher of theology, "everything else in the earthly life of our Lord was unique; it would seem strange if His birth were not." Much as I believe in the Virgin Birth, and in preaching about it, irenically, I should not do so in this series, which already runs too long. In planning a series, as in preparing a sermon, omit anything you cannot illuminate. Stop before anybody begins to wish you would.

Perhaps by its audacity my series impressed the hearers. The attendance kept increasing, and people asked the young dominie to preach about the latter part of the Creed. This he did, later in the year, without passing by a single clause. While he wondered why "communion of saints" came before "forgiveness of sins," he followed the order in the "form of sound words" attributed to the apostles. As for increase of climactic intensity, he found that in each main part of the Creed, the other doctrines led up to eschatology.

The Creed in Christian Experience
Sermons on the Latter Part of the Apostles' Creed

The Truth of the Trinity Today—Matt. 28:19
The Power of the Holy Spirit—Acts 1:8
The Meaning of the Holy Catholic Church—Eph. 3:15
The Fellowship with Saints in Glory—Eph. 3:15
The Promise of God's Forgiveness—I John 1:9
The Resurrection of the Body—I Cor. 15:44

The Facts About the Life Hereafter—John 11:25
The Joys of Heaven as Home—John 14:2

The two series may leave a sense of incompleteness. On the same level of Christian truth a pastor can think of other doctrines that laymen ought to put into their living creed. The subjects that follow might form two series, each with four sermons, and a gap between the two series. Here again, the climactic element has to do with the hereafter.

Additions to the Apostles' Creed

   I. The Bible as God's Written Word—II Tim. 3:15
  II. The Bible Teaching About Man—Ps. 8:4
 III. The Meaning of Our Worship—John 4:24
 IV. The Power of Christian Prayer—Jas. 5:16b
  V. The Pattern of Christian Service—John 13:15
 VI. The Romance of World Missions—Isa. 11:9b
VII. The Bible Vision of World Peace—Mic. 4:2-4
VIII. The Future of God's Kingdom—Rev. 11:15

In a series all the topics may follow much the same pattern, with similar phrasing because of like substance. But a preacher should not use the same pattern too often, or too continuously, lest his handiwork call attention to itself. Without any direct reference to the Creed, Arthur J. Moore shows how to phrase parallel subjects with skill. In his book *The Mighty Saviour* [2] the first message has to do with the divine aspects of our Lord's Person. Then follow nine subjects, which I have broken into two series, one for the four Sundays in Advent and the other for five weekday evenings in Holy Week. Without distortion I have altered a few subjects, which all point to *The Mighty Saviour.*

---

[2] New York and Nashville: Abingdon Press, 1952.

The Love That Sent Him—Rev. 1:5
The Anthem That Announced Him—Luke 2:14
The Name That Was Given Him—Matt. 1:21
The Mission That Brought Him—Luke 19:10

The Cross Where They Crucified Him—I Cor. 2:2
The Decision We Make About Him—Matt. 27:22
The Freedom Sinners Find in Him—John 8:28
The Credentials of a Life for Him—Gal. 6:17
The Home Where We Shall Dwell with Him—John 14:1-3

STRESSING DISTINCTIVE BELIEFS

Brooks used to say that in the Lord's garden each bed of flowers had a beauty and a fragrance of its own. He would have felt a sense of loss if someone had scrambled the flowers so as to obscure the modesty of violets, the vividness of roses, the stateliness of chrysanthemums, and the splendor of gladioli. In apostolic days, according to B. H. Streeter and other New Testament scholars, Christian churches were called to be one in the Lord, but not with dull, drab sameness. "Where the Spirit of the Lord is, there is liberty" (II Cor. 3:17). Whatever the future may hold in the way of church union, may no body of believers ever lose sight of its own distinctive beliefs.

Lutheran ministers ought to preach on what they believe about the Lord's Supper. One summer at Maywood Seminary, Chicago, I taught with professors representing four branches of Lutheranism, which I hope will soon become one. In conversation I learned that none of the four held what we Presbyterians called "the Lutheran theory of the Lord's Supper." Neither did I believe what they termed "the Presbyterian theory." We five professors expressed our beliefs in various ways, but at heart we came close together, rejoicing in the spiritual presence of Christ at His Table. I wonder how many

101

Lutheran, or Presbyterian, laymen have ever heard a teaching sermon directly on this subject.

Presbyterians hold to the doctrine of predestination, about which outsiders often say things that sound strange to us. In a sermon with this subject, "Predestination," a former book editor tells laymen what he as a middle-of-the-road man here believes. If he started with a topic about God's providence, he might preach the sermon in a non-Presbyterian pulpit and never cause a ripple, save one of satisfaction. The doctrine has nothing to do with fatalism, but tells of "an unconquerable faith, a faith in God's purpose for us so deeply rooted that nothing the world can do to us can turn us aside from it."

"Kagawa . . . was forced once to give up his work because . . . he was in danger of going blind, . . . just at a time when his work, after a long, hard grind, seemed about to meet with success." When a friend lamented Kagawa's misfortune, he replied: "You do not understand. . . . This is not a mischance. Through this time of quiet and darkness God has been doing something with me that he could have done in no other way." "We do not say that God planned for Kagawa to get a serious eye infection, but the event, being met, . . . was lifted up and became a part, an essential part, of the unfolding of God's purpose for Kagawa." [3]

Many pastors serve in bodies that do not subscribe to creeds. Still their people need to learn about the doctrines underlying their distinctive practices. Among Friends, who would not welcome a moving discourse about the meaning of the Inner Light, or about Whittier's hymns, with their message of inner peace? As for larger bodies without formal creeds, Southern Baptist churches have been multiplying more rapidly than any

[3] From *The Recovery of Humanity* by James D. Smart, Copyright, 1953, by W. L. Jenkins, The Westminster Press. Used by permission.

other major group of Protestants. Why? Not least because they rely largely on preaching, much of it directly doctrinal and often at night. In Memphis and environs, as in Birmingham, each with approximately one hundred churches, every one has an evening service the year around, and a midweek meeting. My friends who know the facts inform me that they have heard of nothing else anywhere among Southern Baptist churches.

I asked E. N. Patterson, professor in the Baptist Seminary at New Orleans, to outline a series of doctrinal sermons, about which I can include only two of his comments, all illuminating. Modestly he said at first: "Since Baptists do not have a creed, no person can say what all Baptists believe. . . . These subjects show what doctrines most Baptists hold." With a few changes the statement would show what many Disciples of Christ believe.

WHAT BAPTISTS BELIEVE ABOUT GREAT DOCTRINES

The Bible as God's Revelation to Men—II Tim. 3:16
God as Absolute Sovereign Over All Creation—Rom. 8:28-30
Every Person Coming Into the World Born a Sinner—Rom. 3:23
Christ the Sacrifice for the Sin of the World—Heb. 9:22
Saved Forever—John 10:27-28
The Church Christ Is Building—Matt. 16:18
Ye Shall Live Forever—Luke 16:19-31
Christ Is Coming Again—I Thess. 4:13-18

What about "believers' baptism"? That falls under the teaching about the church, a term that refers to a local congregation. Note Patterson's stress on the New Testament:

We believe that a New Testament church is a group of believers in Christ, going with Him after the lost. . . . That a New Testament church has two simple ordinances, which have no sacramental value, but are symbolical in meaning: (1) Baptism by immersion, presenting the death and burial of the old man of sin, and the resurrection of the new man in Christ, to walk in newness of life. (2) The Lord's Supper as presenting to us the shed blood of Christ, who died for our sins. . . . A New Testament church has two types of ordained servants: (1) Pastor or bishop; in the New Testament the terms are used interchangeably. (2) Deacon. We do not believe that in a New Testament church any officer has any more authority than any other member of the church.

RESTRICTING THE FIELD OF VIEW

A pastor may wish to restrict the scope of a series. Instead of preaching about a succession of subjects, each with a sermon of its own, he may set apart a month to consider "The Meaning of God in Christian Experience." The texts may come from the Fourth Gospel, which abounds in doctrine. In the church bulletin, and in other publicity, he may ask the friends to read this Gospel and pray for the services.

    I. The Meaning of God as Life (1:4a)
   II. The Glory of God as Light (1:4b)
  III. The Goodness of God as Love (3:16)
  IV. The Unveiling of God in Christ (14:9a)
   V. The Nearness of God as Father (14:9b)

Despite the simplicity in form, the series may prove difficult to prepare. Who can define or describe such a word as life or love? Paul Tillich, of Harvard, one of the ablest philosopher-theologians, declares: "I have given no definition of love. This is impossible because there is no higher principle by which it could be defined. It is life itself in its actual unity. The forms and structures in which love embodies itself are the forms and structures in which life . . . overcomes its self-destructive forces." [4] At the same university a learned sociologist, not a professing Christian, has an encyclopedic volume about love in world religions. Pitirim A. Sorokin writes: "Love is the heart and soul of ethical goodness. . . . God is love, and love is God. Without love there is no morality and no religion. If this stream of love in religion or ethics ever dries up, both become empty and dead." [5]

The spirit of love emerges in a "series of meditations for apostles of sensitiveness." Howard Thurman here pays homage to the late scholar Dean Edward I. Bosworth, of Oberlin. During a Thanksgiving service at Old First Church, Bosworth heard an aged Negro woman give her testimony. At sixty-two years of age she had learned to read so as to enjoy her Bible. Rising to speak, she felt overcome by emotion. Soon she gained self-control; and then she said, simply: "I know that my redeemer lives, for he lives in my soul. Glory Hallelujah!" There followed a breathless silence. Into the stillness came the voice of Bosworth, another saint: "What the sister has just said is the final word that the human spirit has to say about the meaning of life and the meaning of God. . . . I can only repeat her words, 'I know that my redeemer lives, for he lives in my soul. Glory Hallelujah!' " [6]

Another Christian mystic, D. T. Niles, writes from India, his native land:

I am a sinner for whom Christ died. I am just one of those who have been loved by God in Christ at the Cross. That is the central truth about me. All the rest is peripheral. I am a minister. . . . I have written and published some books. I am son and husband and father and friend, but none of these are me. I myself am

---

[4] The Protestant Era (University of Chicago Press, 1948), p. 160.
[5] The Ways and Power of Love (Boston: Beacon Press, 1954), pp. 78-79.
[6] Deep Is the Hunger (New York: Harper & Bros., 1951), p. 159.

simply he whose death God has encompassed. When a man meets with God and is defeated by Him, then has begun for him the victorious life. He must learn to live by this love with which we are loved. Only so do we live at all, for we live most deeply when we live in the passive voice.[7]

PREPARING AN INFORMAL COURSE

A wise man preaches serially only at intervals. In a downtown church serial preaching may flourish, perennially. Elsewhere a pastor may have only three or four series a year, with no two as close neighbors. In between any two special series he can have what I call a course. I mean a number of consecutive sermons on the same general subject, but not prepared or announced as a unified series. Usually I did my serial preaching at night, to attract hearers. I preached course after course at the morning hour, in a sanctuary normally filled to overflowing.

The idea of preaching a course I owe to R. W. Dale. Just before one Easter Day, as every reader knows, he discovered the fact of the living Christ. Then his heart began to burn,

> Like some watcher of the skies
> When a new planet swims into his ken.

Week after week Dale kept preaching about Christ as living now and as with us here. In his Yale Lectures, on the basis of such experiences, he declared:

We can hardly preach too often on any subject by which we ourselves are deeply moved. We may return to it Sunday after Sunday and month after month. . . . Never be afraid of saying the same thing over and over again, if you feel driven to say it by a strong

[7] From *Preaching the Gospel of the Resurrection*, by D. T. Niles, 1953, The Westminster Press. Used by permission.

sense of its importance. . . . Most preachers who have any life and passion in them are under the benignant despotism of a succession of great truths and facts during successive periods of their ministry.[8]

This counsel heartened me to begin a course about the Incarnation. I had been schooled to stress the Atonement, but not much else about Christ, as divine. From Dale I learned that "in studying any doctrine it is well to begin with the history." So I went through a historical book, The Doctrine of the Incarnation (1896), by R. L. Ottley, and then a doctrinal one, The Incarnation of the Son of God (1891), by Charles Gore—two works, quite different, which I recommend as easy to follow. Of course I strove also to master the biblical teachings about the Incarnation. When the reservoir began to overflow, I started to preach my course, not knowing how long I could continue. For thirteen Sunday mornings I spoke on various aspects of the "Incarnation in Our City," with never a reference to more than the one sermon in hand or in view.

In starting that course, like Abraham, by faith I went out, not knowing whither, but knowing why. I wish that I could recapture the spirit of wonder and awe with which I led the people into a "promised land" as new and strange to them as it had been to me twelve months before. Later I did the reading that led to a dozen messages about "Reconciliation Through the Cross," and after that "The Gospel of the Resurrection." Never did the idea of a course get beyond my study. The stress each time fell on one sermon in its own right. The Lord must have kept me from calling attention to how I was preaching, but never from stressing some aspect of the doctrine

[8] Nine Lectures on Preaching (London: Hodder & Stoughton, Ltd., 1898), pp. 122-23.

that had set my own heart aflame. I wish that I could preach that way as a peripatetic professor.

This kind of pulpit work encourages a pastor to read books that he can never forget, and even more, to hold fellowship with the Book that makes men live. Instead of reading up hastily and sketchily on a different subject every week, a man lives with the same books of theology, and with the same book of the Bible, until his reservoir begins to overflow. Then he starts to preach. As long as the reservoir continues to overflow, he can keep on preaching. It will overflow week after week if he keeps on reading and mastering the source books in the spirit of prayer.

PART TWO

Preparing a
Doctrinal Sermon

CHAPTER NINE

THE CHOICE OF
A DOCTRINE TO PREACH

NOW WE COME TO THE MORE DIFFICULT HALF OF THE
subject. We face the preacher's forgotten word, "how?"
Many writers on preaching ignore such things, because they
seem unscholarly. As God's interpreter of doctrine to common
people, what does a good man need most? He should know
what to preach and how to do it well. The spiritual value depends much on his knowing what; the popular effectiveness,
more on his knowing how. First of all, if he is well grounded in
Christian doctrine, how should a man decide which truth to
preach next?

ALLOWING TIME FOR MEDITATION

A pastor should review his sermons at least once a year. He
may find that they fall into two groups: those that inspire and
those that inform. As for the difference, he can sense it, but
scarcely describe it. A man with a certain bent has to guard
against trying to inspire all the time, lest his laymen learn next
to nothing. Even in a Mickey Mouse program for children,
Walt Disney plans for "entertainment dealing with factual
subjects." A minister with a serious mind may always strive
to inform, with no glimpse of heights to which the hearers
ought to soar, feeling "lost in wonder, love, and praise."

By thinking and praying about these matters, a pastor can
keep out of self-made ruts. Without following hard-and-fast
rules, he can decide what the people need at a given season and

111

in each sermon. "Not necessarily what they consciously want," says Brooks, but "no more necessarily what they do not want." A wise man keeps in view the occasion, the interests of the hearers, and the ability of the interpreter. Within these limits he ought to preach whatever most warms his own heart.

In choosing a doctrine, give the preference to one about which you have been thinking for a while, the longer the better. Unlike a mushroom, a teaching message does not spring out of the ground overnight, full-grown. The final form may come to view not long before you write it out in full, or make an extensive outline. The completed sermon ought to embody the ripened fruit of reading, thinking, and praying over a period long enough for the germinal idea to mature. Like a sonnet or a statue, the idea of a sermon comes to its best after a period of "subconscious incubation."

Take the statue of Brooks, which stands beside Trinity Church in Boston. Before Saint-Gaudens made the final drawings, he had kept the project in mind ten years. At one stage he had intended to show an angel towering over the form of Brooks. Later the sculptor let the figure of the living Christ dominate the statue, because He had dominated the life of the beloved pastor. Some reader may protest that in preparing a sermon he does not have ten years, or ten days, to prepare. No, not unless he has learned to plan his pulpit work. While in the seminary young Brooks started to jot down fugitive ideas, "flashes in the world of thought," which later resulted in sermons. While reading one of the Church Fathers, or walking over the Virginia hills, he saw visions of truth, which he caught on the wing before they could fly away and be lost.[1]

[1] See A. V. G. Allen, *Life and Letters of Phillips Brooks* (New York: E. P. Dutton & Co., 1910), I, 178-96.

After a man catches an "illuminating flash," he may have to wait for months before the sermon begins to assume a form that anyone else can see. Meanwhile the new conception needs as careful nurture as a babe in a mother's womb. If properly fed with truth from a Bible book and from other works, the idea will keep growing. In fact, it may call for more than one sermon. During the first year or two in the seminary, this way of working may seem fantastic; but this is the way the masters of the art have let their sermons grow—men as different as Brooks and Beecher, F. W. Robertson and C. H. Spurgeon. This statement any advanced student can verify by going to the original sources about each pulpit master's ways of study. Please do not call him a "great preacher"! He has a great Gospel and a great God.

Such a description may prove misleading. It stresses the need for watchful waiting, first to conceive the idea, and then to wait for its birth, at a time no one can predict in advance. The period of waiting does not consist in idle romance. Think of the work involved. If at the end there comes a message to help and uplift God's people, who can object to drudgery and weariness along the way? In writing about the life hereafter, Edward I. Bosworth has a word picture that anyone with imagination can apply to preaching. The Oberlin divine has been speaking about our coming to the glories of the hereafter "through peril, toil and pain":

When a man has walked all day up the valley of the Visp, and finally sees the Matterhorn rising in quiet majesty into the unfolding sky, he forgets about the blisters on his foot. The daily practice of immortality makes the small frictions of life seem to be the small things they really are. The mountains of eternity cast the spell of their daily peace over his life.[2]

[2] Ernest Pye, *The Biography of a Mind: Bosworth of Oberlin* (New York: Bosworth Memorial Fund, 1948), p. 72.

What the English biographer of Florence Nightingale says about biography applies equally well to preaching:

> There has to be a flash in which the possibilities of a subject burst on the writer like a revelation—"I never understood! I never realized!" . . . the writer will declare to himself. He will be excited, filled with missionary zeal, a man with a cause. [And he will work with joy.] . . . Without the flash, without the missionary zeal and the obsession which follows, . . . no satisfactory biography can be written.[3]

What an ideal!

A hard-working sermon builder may exclaim: "You talk about an illuminating flash and shivers of joy running up a man's back. I never have had anything of the sort. To me the making of sermons means drudgery, not delight." Except for a person with genius, every young craftsman must learn how to handle his tools; but after a time of apprenticeship, perhaps in the seminary, anyone called to prepare sermons can learn a "more excellent way" than that of wielding hammer and ax, or using scissors and paste. A preacher sent from God uses brains and imagination, mingled with faith and hope, and joy ever in the offing. So with what Jowett calls "apostolic optimism," let us turn directly to the subject "How decide which doctrine to preach next?"

KEEPING ON THE MAIN TRACK

John Henry Jowett says:

> We must grapple with the big things, the things about which our people will hear nowhere else; the deep, the abiding, the things that permanently matter. We are not appointed merely

[3] Cecil Woodham-Smith, "Biographies I'd Like to Write and Never Shall," *New York Times Book Review*, July 24, 1955, p. 7.

to give good advice, but to proclaim good news. Therefore must the apostolic themes be our themes: The holiness of God; the love of God; the grace of the Lord Jesus; the solemn wonders of the cross; the ministry of the Divine forgiveness; the fellowship of His sufferings; the power of the Resurrection; the blessedness of divine communion; the heavenly places in Christ Jesus; the mystical indwelling of the Holy Ghost; the abolition of the deadliness of death; the ageless life; our Father's house; the liberty of the glory of the children of God.[4]

Anyone can add to the list, but no one ought to take away from it. In making his list, Jowett kept on the main track of revealed truth. A man of another sort might have included such side issues as "heavenly recognition" and "the authorship of the Epistle to the Hebrews." Jowett never preached a sermon on either subject. He believed in heavenly recognition, and he would not object to a paragraph or two about the matter. He felt sure that Paul did not write the letter to the Hebrews, but Jowett knew that such matters of criticism have no place in the pulpit. "A doctrine is an intellectual formulation of an experience," and no interpreter has time to preach about things that do not matter tremendously.

On the main highway think of God's perseverance. Usually we stress His providence, which undergirds everything good. So does God's perseverance. If the aim was inspirational, the sermon could grow out of an inspiring text such as: "Hast thou not known? hast thou not heard, that the everlasting God, the Lord, the Creator of the ends of the earth, fainteth not, neither is weary?" (Isa. 40:28). Here, and in the still more majestic words that follow, the prophet is not teaching a truth, but is inspiring persons who find life full of drudgery, shadowed

---

[4] *The Preacher, His Life and Work* (New York: George H. Doran Co., 1912), pp. 100-101. Used by permission of Harper & Bros.

by despair. A more doctrinal sermon may grow out of a teaching text. In writing from a prison at Rome the Apostle teaches much the same truth: "The One Who has begun His good work in you will go on developing it until the Day of Jesus Christ" (Phil. 1:6).[5]

In dealing with such a verse, a man should keep on the main highway, according to his purpose. If he wishes to explain the passage, he may teach something about the Bible book, and more about the prayer in which the text appears, with much about "the Day" at the end of the present age. All these materials, proper in an expository message, a doctrinal sermon may leave untouched and unnoticed, in order to fix attention on one truth, "The God Who Perseveres." In line with the text from Philippians, a sermon may follow the order of time: the God of yesterday, of today, and of tomorrow. He never lets up; He never lets down; He never lets go. "From everlasting to everlasting, God." No wonder Sidney Lanier could sing:

> As the marsh-hen secretly builds on the watery sod,
> Behold I will build me a nest on the greatness of God.
> .   .   .   .
> By so many roots as the marsh-grass sends in the sod
> I will heartily lay me a-hold on the greatness of God.[6]

In order to keep on the main track from week to week, one need only follow the Christian Year. Many of us serve in churches that do not prescribe such ways of worship, but any pastor can follow this historic guide in determining which

---

[5] J. B. Phillips, *Letters to Young Churches.* Copyright 1947 by The Macmillan Co. and used by their permission.

[6] From "The Marshes of Glynn."

doctrines to preach. In making his list of pulpit "musts," Jowett did not begin with Advent and build up toward eternity; but still his subjects accorded with the Christian Year. In following this trail no minister need feel ashamed and try to preach by the Christian calendar, surreptitiously.

Like Jowett, G. Campbell Morgan did not lead in public worship according to prescribed forms, but in the pulpit he showed awareness of untold preaching values in the Christian Year. At the beginning of Advent he once said:

We are now approaching the festival of Christmas. I am proposing to speak for four successive Sundays on the purposes of the Advent. The importance of the subject cannot be overstated. The whole teaching of Holy Scripture places the Advent at the center of the methods of God with a sinning race. It is surely important therefore that we understand its purposes in the economy of God.

Sermon topics: "To Destroy the Works of the Devil" (I John 3:8); "To Take Away Our Sins" (I John 3:5); "To Reveal the Father" (John 14:9); "To Prepare for a Second Advent" (Heb. 9:28).

Another interpreter might single out other aspects of the Incarnation. As a popular preacher Morgan often did the unexpected. Where one would start with "The Revealing of the Father," Morgan began with a truth sure to attract attention, as the devil always does. Surely the preacher did well to close with eschatology. What concerns us now is the fact that in planning to preach from the home pulpit he gave much heed to the Christian Year. In any one sermon he did not try to tell all he knew about the Incarnation. Once in youth I did that and made no impression for good. Now I should have an Advent series on "The Incarnation: Good News for Busy

117

Men." Topics: "Good News About God Our Father" (John 14:9); ". . . About Us Men" (1:14); ". . . About Our Sins" (1:29); ". . . About Our Service" (13:3-4). This last would be "The Gospel of the Towel."

Some year for variety deal with four sayings from that many church worthies. Each sermon would have a Bible text, as interpreted by the chosen saying, which would provide the motif of the message. The motif saying would come immediately after the text and sound out at times through the sermon.

I. "He came to save every age," said Irenaeus (d. cir. 202); "therefore He came as an infant, a child, a boy, a youth, and a man."

II. "He became human," said Athanasius (d. 373), "that we might become divine."

III. "Nothing arouses a great soul to the performance of good deeds," said Chrysostom (d. 407), "so much as learning that in this it is like God."

IV. "All that is divine in Him is human," said James Denney (d. 1917), "and all that is human is divine."

In each case an interpreter ought to read at least one book by the author concerned, not to secure preaching materials, but to get the "feel" of the subject. After such teaching messages for a month, the lay hearer should have a new sense of the riches in the truth he celebrates at Christmas, and a new spirit of wonder when he sings with Charles Wesley:

> Veiled in flesh the Godhead see,
> Hail th' incarnate Deity!

PLANNING TO BE SPECIFIC

Gradually a pastor learns to preach about large subjects, each of them momentous, but with only a single important aspect in a sermon. According to John Henry Newman in his *The Idea of a University Defined*, pastoral preaching ought usually to be specific. A brilliant peripatetic divine can paint each time on a vast canvas, as Tintoretto and Veronese did at Florence. That kind of art is easier to admire than to remember. A pastor as preacher does more good by dealing practically with one aspect of a mighty truth, and by fashioning a cameo that every beholder can recall with delight. A French oratorical preacher, such as Bourdaloue or Massillon, could charm licentious royal hearers with "great sermons" which did not deter them from sinning. A local interpreter helps ordinary people more by preaching "good sermons." This means pulpit work that leads the hearer Godward.

Such a way of preparing sermons calls for much more than pious intentions. A man full of zeal may attempt too much at a time. Into a single discourse he may crush references to nearly all the basic Christian doctrines, as much mixed up as an old-fashioned pickle compiled in autumn and labeled the "tail end of the garden." Personally I prefer a cucumber pickle unmixed and not too sour. Even when a person confines himself to a single truth, he may make it seem dull, heavy, and hard to digest. What a way to misrepresent God and the wonders of redemption! The fault usually lies in making an omnibus concoction with enough half-cooked ideas for four Sunday dinners.

A sermon sound in doctrine but lifeless as a log comes from an able man of yesterday. Instead of singling out one aspect of the Incarnation, such as the idea he puts last, this man has four main truths, with nothing to show the underlying unity. The sermon begins with a royal text (John 1:14), which the topic does little to interpret. Subject: "The Incarnation." The introduction, being conventional, does not concern us now.

The sermon proper falls into these parts, all true:

    I. The Person spoken of—the Word
   II. The affirmation—made flesh
  III. The proof—"we beheld his glory"
  IV. The results that flow from this reality.[7]

That was how many of us were taught to preach doctrine before we quit making sermons that showed everything about the Incarnation except the meaning, the value, and the glory. From such a liberal evangelical as George A. Gordon of Boston we orthodox young men could have learned to use imagination, and never to preach a sermon that we could not see. At New Old South Church, Gordon once dealt with the Incarnation (John 1:14) as God's answer to the question "What is the meaning of the life of Jesus?"

The Incarnation is the meaning of the life of Jesus. . . . There is no theory about Jesus that will do justice to the facts except that which finds in his advent the advent of the Soul of God. . . . Like an inverted rainbow was the Soul of the Lord, coming down out of heaven, returning into heaven, and revealing in its whole sacred curve the beauty of the Eternal Light, the glory of the Infinite Father.[8]

I can see that "inverted rainbow" and what it shows about Christ. So can I see what James S. Stewart says about the humanity of Christ. In a sermon (Matt. 21:10) "Behold the Man," Stewart declares:

Incomparably the most important watershed in the long history of humanity has been the Incarnation. . . . Who is this Jesus? The deeper answer to that question we must hold over for our next study [Col. 2:9]. We shall consider then . . . the sublime and

---

[7] William Taylor, op. cit., pp. 15-29.
[8] Revelation and the Ideal (Boston: Houghton Mifflin Co., 1913), p. 254.

breathtaking conviction of the men of the New Testament, that this Jesus was God manifest in the flesh. But for the present let us concentrate on getting this one thing quite clear—that whoever and whatever else He may have been, . . . He was at least *truly and fully man.*

I beg you never to let that go. It is crucial for salvation. If Jesus was not truly a man, if His humanity was in some sense unreal, an appearance or a disguise, if the Figure in the Gospels was an unearthly angelic visitant, a demigod in human shape, the whole doctrine of redemption falls to the ground. Hold on to the full humanity of Jesus! [9]

Note the limiting of the field. See also that specific preaching need not result in Lilliputian sermonettes about the fringe of the Master's seamless robe. Whatever the chosen aspect of the Incarnation, both speaker and hearer ought to see more than a little of the doctrine as a whole. For example, think about the practical subject "What It Means to Be a Christian." One of many answers comes from words of Paul about the Incarnation: "Let this mind be in you, which was also in Christ Jesus" (Phil. 2:5). The introduction could bring out the meaning of the word Christian: being like our Lord in the days of His flesh. From this point of view the text in its background shows three facts. Being a Christian

    I. Calls for a spirit of humility.
    II. Leads to a life of service.
    III. Issues in readiness to sacrifice.

Like other skeletons, this one looks lifeless. The resulting sermon ought to teem with life and action. Even the least distinguished hearer ought to see that by God's grace he can

[9] *The Strong Name* (New York: Charles Scribner's Sons, 1941), pp. 69, 75-76. Used by permission of the publisher.

become like the King of Glory in the most divine thing the Redeemer ever has done. The truth here calls, not for mechanistic imitation of Christ, but for living in Him by faith. According to this "prison epistle" being a Christian means to be in Christ, with a motive power like the one that brought Him to earth, filled His ministry in Galilee, and led Him to the Cross.

EMPLOYING TECHNICAL TERMS

Is it wise to use in the pulpit such a technical term as "Incarnation"? The word does not appear in the Bible and does not interest most laymen. As a rule a pastor-preacher should not talk in technical terms, which seem to laymen abstract and impersonal. In a doctrinal sermon, however, one such word may have to appear, and that quite often. Either the pulpit should fill such a term as "Incarnation" with old light and new meaning, or else the Church ought to discard its historic vocabulary. To discard it now would look strangely like forsaking the Christianity of the New Testament. So let us translate every such word into thought-forms of our day, but with only one abstract term in each doctrinal sermon.

In our day of increased specialization, and with the growing prestige of science, the minister may be the only professional man in town who seriously considers giving up the technical terms of his calling. A research chemist writes a routine report full of polysyllables that make an outside reader feel dizzy. A physician talks about "syncope," "syndrome," and many other such things remote from the thinking of the man in the street. A lawyer has his "torts," with "cases in equity," and phrases about "tenancy by entireties." And yet a specialist in internal medicine can tell an ordinary man all he needs to know about

122

his incipient coronary condition. So can a lawyer address a jury of a dozen men and women, using a technical term whenever necessary, and win a favorable verdict.

When the members of a jury come to church, they expect the minister to know the technical terms of his calling, and without apology to use one of them whenever the facts warrant. They respect a man who knows his Bible in the original languages, especially if he can read Latin and German. They do not wish him to parade his erudition or to hide his learning under a bushel of Uriah Heep " 'umility." When they hear a sermon about the Incarnation, they like to know that the word comes from a Latin root meaning "being clothed with flesh." Some people still care for Latin; and everybody knows that there is such a language, "dead" until somebody brings it back to life.

At the National Museum in Cairo the curator showed a group of us how to make relics from antiquity seem alive and full of meaning. After he had explained the treasures from the tomb of King Tutankhamen, he called our attention to a large vase not at all attractive. He explained that it had no archaeological value and no historical significance. Still he kept looking at it with pride like that of a man gazing down at his first granddaughter. After the curator had let us puzzle our brains, he reached down into the vase and turned on an electric light. Then the glory of God shone out through what proved to be, not a vessel of comon clay, but a piece of alabaster.

Preaching the Gospel of the Incarnation calls for some such artistry, which differs far from showmanship. A preacher must have in hand a truth full of meaning and beauty, and the ability to get people interested, it may be by appealing to curiosity. He should be able, at will, to turn on an inner light and to keep it burning. Then the doctrine with an impersonal name will begin to glow with a radiance from above. If any man lacks the ability to illuminate a truth of God, he should not attempt to prepare a doctrinal sermon. On the other hand, if the local curator of God's treasure house lives among these truths year after year, he will find a way to turn on that inner light.

CHAPTER TEN

THE TREATMENT
OF A BIBLE PASSAGE

THE PREPARATION OF A DOCTRINAL SERMON MAY
begin with mastery of a Bible passage. The choice of a
subject ought to come from a sense of local needs. That affords
a practical purpose to guide in studying a passage written to
meet the end in view. I am not now referring to Bible exposition. Expository work should have a large place in the pulpit,
but there is a difference between the exposition of a Bible
passage and the preaching of a Bible doctrine. The hearer cannot remember both the Bible exposition and the doctrinal
explanation equally well. Alexander Maclaren's laymen, for
example, learned much from his Bible expositions but little
about Christian doctrine. Dale's hearers learned much about
Christian doctrine but not much about any Bible passage.
Here let us think about making approximately half of a man's
pulpit work doctrinal.

PREACHING IN THE HARVEST SEASON

In a typical congregation the time between Christmas and
Easter forms the harvest season, the best period for ingathering
converts. In addition to sermons that show the meaning of
passages in the life of our Lord, a pastor may have doctrinal
sermons about the Kingdom. Since people are thinking in
terms of the Gospels, he can turn to Matthew, with its stress
on the Kingdom. The Sunday before New Year's may call for
a text to serve as a church motto during the next twelve

months. "Thy kingdom come. Thy will be done in earth, as it is in heaven" (6:10). These words voice a prayer for today and tomorrow. Postponing until later such matters as missions, world peace, and eschatology, the minister can stress the motto as it concerns the local church this next year.

With such a practical aim, and such a golden text, the minister in his workshop has a project full of fascination. Starting with the Greek Testament, he looks on the text as an integral part of the Lord's Prayer and of the First Gospel. Of course he consults standard commentaries, and books about the meaning of the Kingdom, notably one by John Bright, *The Kingdom of God*. Gradually the pastor learns what the text has to say in its own Bible setting. The details of exegesis need not appear in the sermon, any more than a surgeon's knowledge of anatomy appears when he performs an operation. So let us assume that a fresh study of the Bible passage and related books leads to a message about "The Kingdom of God in Our Church Next Year."

The Kingdom
    I. Means the place where God has His way.
    II. Calls for people glad to do His will.
    III. Comes through prayer for His blessing.

Earlier in the century we preached about "ushering in the Kingdom." It seemed to tarry just around the corner and to wait for us introducers. In "songs of praise," not praise to God, we exhorted one another:

> His Kingdom tarries long;
> Bring in the day of brotherhood
> And end the night of wrong.[1]

[1] William P. Merrill. Used by permission of *The Presbyterian Tribune*.

Even the women, who usually know better about things spiritual, joined the ranks of Kingdom bringers. A major denomination of New Jersey adopted as a motto for the year's work in world missions: "It All Depends on Me!" While we were singing and praying about the world's growing better and better day by day, because we had come on the scene, hell burst loose in a global war. Looking back we now feel like falling on our faces and confessing that in our century we have not solved a single major ethical problem. We have failed to bring in the Kingdom by doing away with war, racial strife, the liquor traffic, commercialized vice, legalized gambling, and other such agencies of the devil.

When the Kingdom comes, as come it will, we shall ascribe the power and the glory to God. "Not unto us, O Lord, not unto us, but unto thy name give glory." Once a friend spoke to Mary Slessor of Calabar about the coming stars in her crown. That noblest of women missionaries replied: "What could I do with a starry crown but cast it at the feet of my Redeemer?" All the while, in the spirit of our motto text, she strove to lead others in doing the will of God, who had called her to pray because the coming of the Kingdom depended on Him, and to work as though it all depended on her.

"When Jesus came preaching," He always spoke about the Kingdom. Sometimes He dealt with the idea broadly; more often, with reference to something specific, such as children in the home. In His "Kingdom Teachings," some of which we once labeled "social," the stress usually falls on one person. The same motif sounds out in the closing lecture of Brooks at Yale: "The Value of the Human Soul." What here follows does not come from Brooks, but from the exegetical study of a Bible passage. "What is a man profited, if he shall gain the whole world, and lose his own soul?" (Matt. 16:26). Subject:

"The Value of Your Soul." A study in profit and loss, with Christ as the Appraiser. He says that your soul

    I. Means all in you that is Godlike.
   II. Is worth more than all the things on earth.
  III. May lose its likeness to God.
  IV. Can be restored through faith in Christ.

Brooks always started a sermon with a text. Whenever a minister does so, he ought to let the tone color of the text determine the tone color of the sermon. Tone color here means the distinctive quality that makes a preaching text differ from almost everything else in the Bible. Because of poor teaching, many a man has spent three years in a divinity school without learning how to sense the tone color of a Bible text. The ablest book on *The Art of Teaching* [2] says that A. E. Housman, an English poet-professor, spent his life lecturing about beautiful Latin poetry without calling attention to its beauty. That sounds like the way seminary professors used to teach the far richer beauty of the Bible.

A preacher poorly trained may not even try to teach what his passage means. A well-known clergyman has in print a sermon in answer to an indirect question: "What It Means to Be a Christian." He starts with an admirable text, to which he pays no attention, a text that begins: "I am crucified with Christ" (Gal. 2:20). If I were a layman seeking a better life, I should feel bewildered by the three answers—each of them true negatively. Being a Christian, says the sermon, does not mean

    I. Simply to be a good man.
   II. Necessarily to believe a certain creed.
  III. Once to have experienced "Conversion."

[2] By Gilbert Highet (New York: Alfred A. Knopf, Inc., 1950), p. 226.

"Is that all? Is there no Good News for me as a sinner?" The brother may not have had time to master his text, which is difficult. If so, he should have left it out of the sermon. Better still, by resorting to exegesis he could have shown the meaning of Christian experience in the light of the Cross. Alas, a minister who follows the modern fashion of discussing a positive subject negatively may do it so often as to forget what P. T. Forsyth proclaimed about *Positive Preaching and the Modern Mind.* Norman Vincent Peale has a far different emphasis, scarcely doctrinal; but the amazing popularity of his book *The Power of Positive Thinking* shows that countless people have become fed up with present-day pulpit negations.

KEEPING TO ONE PASSAGE

Let every sermon have its text, only one text, with its setting. In the coming discourse, forsaking all other texts, cleave to one. In other days, when churchgoers knew something about the Bible, Spurgeon preached an acceptable sermon with seven texts, widely scattered through the Scriptures. Each of the seven consisted of the same words: "I have sinned" (Luke 15:21b et al.). Today churchgoers find it far easier to follow one text, in its background. Fosdick seems at times to work from this point of view. Often he does not start a sermon with a text, but he may bring one out a little later. Once at Christmas he began with the subject "The Modern World's Discovery of Sin." Soon he referred to a Christmas text: "Thou shalt call his name Jesus: for he shall save his people from their sins" (Matt. 1:21). This text he did not explain, but still he showed an understanding of it and an appreciation of its tone color.

In a fashion still more searching, Fosdick preaches about

"Forgiveness of Sins." [3] He starts by showing that everyone in church should look on himself as a sinner, with sins of temperament, of social attitude, and of neglect. The body of the sermon deals with the difficulty of forgiveness. This truth appears in a text: "Whether is it easier to say to the sick of the palsy, Thy sins be forgiven thee; or to say, Arise, and take up thy bed?" (Mark 2:9). Either of these sermons would evoke criticism from certain quarters. In all fairness let us grant that whenever this man introduces a text, he tries to deal with it fairly. He never uses it to confuse his hearers.

Unintentionally, much so-called doctrinal preaching does confuse. Without opening his Bible or racking his brains, a pastor can make ready to "preach" on "What We Mean by Sin." "Sin is not a figment of the imagination"; "not merely a matter of psychology"; not this, that, or the other—until the time runs out. The hearer finds it hard to follow such a sky pilot, who seems to be flying blind, with no chart, compass, or destination. What does he have but gall? As for the remedy, he needs the self-discipline that comes through mastering a Bible passage every week.

A Bible-believing minister of a different type reports: "I rely on my concordance, a book worth its weight in platinum." Turning to the word "sin," he jots down a number of texts and goes into the pulpit to make running comments about sin as it stands out in each text. When Spurgeon conducted something like a Cook's Tour through Holy Writ, he could do much good. From many another man, not well prepared, such a pulpit effort makes no permanent impression. Where there is not time enough to bring out and illuminate the truth in one text and its background, why deal with half a dozen? Of course

[3] *The Secret of Victorious Living* (New York: Harper & Bros., 1934), pp. 110-19.

a well-known preacher sometimes announces more texts than one; but he uses them as mottoes to be admired, not explained. Motto preaching may do good, but in most hands it soon becomes monotonous.

As a motto for this chapter let me suggest this: "High Fidelity to Holy Writ." Lovers of music can make the proper adjustments; I am addressing lovers of the Bible. For example, take a golden text: "If we confess our sins, he is faithful and just to forgive us our sins, and to cleanse us from all unrighteousness" (I John 1:9). In a textual sermon, not specially doctrinal, a man could preach about three facts of Christian experience, and preferably in this order: confession, forgiveness, cleansing. If so, each term would need to be interpreted, not merely quoted and echoed. Only an expert could do all this in less than twenty-five minutes. At the end of the sermon how many hearers would know what he meant by sin?

"Oh, but 'high fidelity' ought to mean that a man must discuss everything in his text!" Probably so, as a rule, but not always. In the synagogue at Nazareth the Master started with a golden text: "The Spirit of the Lord is upon me" (Luke 4:18; see Isa. 61:1). All at once He stopped in the middle of a verse, using only as much of the passage as suited His purpose. Today, for the sake of lay hearers likely to feel confused, the Lord may wish a minister to omit from a sermon everything not in keeping with his purpose.

Biblical theology shows that the Scriptures do not consist of isolated verses. Except in one book—the main part of Proverbs—the Bible was written with the paragraph as the smallest unit. If an educated minister dealt fairly with seven scattered texts about sin, he would have to deal honorably with seven different paragraphs, in seven Bible books, each with a message and tone color distinctly its own. Why not decide to let every sermon have a single text? Then saturate your soul in the spirit of the text. Since the Psalms tell much about sin, turn to a word picture of "A Mighty Man on His Knees." Someone like King David, a sinner in middle age, is speaking to God: "Against thee, thee only, have I sinned" (51:4a). Sin always starts in the heart of one person, and it always has to do with God. The facts here call for a sermon: "The Meaning of Your Sin."

A week later, "The Forgiveness of Your Sins." In days of war we felt that our foes had sinned en masse. So have we all, but sin concerns each of us; so does forgiveness. The divine Physician does not cure sin-sick souls in squads. His way of working appears in another text about a man like David: "Blessed is he whose transgression is forgiven" (Ps. 32:1). One man and his God! If sin begins in the heart of a man, forgiveness flows from the heart of his God. To a person ashamed and sorry for his sins, the pastor says: Forgiveness means God's way of

    I. Making you right with God Himself.
   II. Leading you to get right with others.
  III. Enabling you to get right with yourself.
  IV. Prompting you to worship God with joy.
   V. Causing you to engage in service.
  VI. Filling you with hopes of heaven.

All true, thank God! But in the spirit of "high fidelity" how many of these truths appear in the text? Only the first! Why not leave the others for later sermons, after the hearer has received God's forgiveness of his sins? One of my favorite book preachers, W. M. Clow, has a sermon that puts too much food on the table. He starts with a simple text: "Through this man is preached unto you the forgiveness of sins" (Acts 13:38).

The sermon discusses God's forgiveness under six headings: It is real—personal—reconciling—fruitful — repeated — and Cross-centered. All true, but hard to remember! Why not leave out two or three courses and take more time to prepare the remaining three or four?

EMPLOYING SCHOLARLY HELPS

I have been assuming what I now wish to stress. "High Fidelity to Holy Writ" calls for a working library of books chosen with care and used every day. Ideally they ought to include commentaries based on the Hebrew and the Greek. One night I was preaching from a part of Isa. 53. Afterward a layman asked if my interpretation agreed with the Septuagint. What if I had never heard about the Greek Version of the Old Testament? In two pews of a sanctuary where he was to preach, a young kinsman found copies of the Greek New Testament. Obviously, some laymen expect a "physician of souls" to know his anatomy and hygiene. Through no fault of his own a pastor may have had little linguistic training. Still he can learn to use scholarly commentaries, so as to interpret Holy Scripture with "high fidelity."

Take "The Meaning of Your Repentance." The hearer may think of repentance as merely turning over a new leaf, not as preparing to start a new life; as giving up bad habits, not as seeking a new heart. In preparing the sermon, a minister need not study all that the Bible and other books teach about repentance; but he should master some one part of the Bible teaching, such as the opening portion of Rom. 2, especially these words: "Do you not know that God's kindness is meant to lead you to repentance?" (vs. 4b R.S.V.). The goodness of God underlies the teaching. On this basis the sermon may show how a person ought to feel about the wrongness inside himself. In view of God's mercies in Christ, "When You Repent," you

I. Feel ashamed of your sins.
II. Learn to hate your sins.
III. Turn from your sins to God.
IV. Set your heart on obeying God.

A case from life shows how the idea once worked. In America we have had no more saintly scholar than Austin Phelps, author of an able guidebook, *The Theory of Preaching*, and a devotional manual, *The Still Hour*. In early boyhood Phelps told a lie, which became known to his father, a saintly minister. Taking the lad into his study, the father broke down and wept. He said that God hated lies and that liars went to hell. The little fellow felt so stricken with grief that he determined never to tell another lie. Years later he declared that in as far as he knew he had kept that vow. Better still, he had learned the meaning of repentance, through the goodness of a father much like God.

In preaching about repentance a pastor needs something more substantial than touching stories. For speedy reference he may use a one-volume commentary, such as Gore's, the *Abingdon*, or the *Twentieth-Century Bible Commentary* (1956), edited by G. H. Davies. On the conservative side, Dummelow's, or the *New Bible Commentary* (1954), edited by Francis Davidson and others. Better still, a pastor needs such a set as the *Expositor's Greek Testament* or the *Interpreter's Bible*, especially the exegetical portions. He ought to have another standard commentary or two on each major book of the Bible. The field here is boundless. A well-trained minister does not need such homiletical helps as Matthew Henry and the *Pulpit Commentary*, which may prove invaluable to a self-taught local preacher.

SOUNDING A CALL TO ACTION

Scholarly books make clear that the kerygma, or New Testament preaching, always sounds a call for repentance. Like the New Testament, these books say little about "The Business of Being Converted." The word "conversion" comes out repeatedly in conversations with laymen. Especially in a community exposed to high-pressure revivalism, people need a sermon on "The Bible Meaning of Conversion." Text: "Except ye be converted, and become as little children, ye shall not enter into the kingdom of heaven" (Matt. 18:3).

In a doctrinal sermon the main stress falls on the meaning of conversion, with less attention to childlikeness. In addressing parents, however, make clear that the Lord does not refer to little children as humble. Show that conversion means

    I. Yielding to an impulse from God.
   II. Turning to God in Christ.
  III. Making a rightabout-face.
  IV. Starting in paths of goodness.

Action, action, action!

Gipsy Smith, Sr., used to say: "Repentance means awaking in the morning; conversion means getting up." A sermon about repentance shows the way a person should feel about sin; one about conversion, how he ought to act. According to the beloved parable, in the "far country" of sin a younger son "came to himself." He felt ashamed and sorry for what he had done. In other words, he repented. Then he turned his back on his evil life and went home to his father, there to confess his sins and plead for pardon. Thus the parable affords a word picture of conversion.

Another sermon may deal with a still more perplexing truth: "The New Birth," or as it reads in the Greek, "The Birth from Above." Text: "No one can see God's Realm unless he is born from above" (John 3:3b Moffatt). As Moody used to say, "The only way to get into God's family is to be born into it." The sermon may deal with "The New Birth: The Beginning of a New Life."

  I. The need for a new beginning
 II. The new beginning from above
III. The birth from above as a mystery
 IV. The mystery as a fact of experience

In this kind of interlocking structure each main part leads up to the next.

After the sermon the mystery may seem deeper. Like Nicodemus, the hearer may ask: "How can these things be?" Then the minister may refer to the wind. No one who has lived on a prairie in the Middle West ever tries to account for the wind. Still less can anyone explain the workings of the Spirit in bringing a soul into new life, but every pastor should know the fact through personal experience and through ministering to others. According to a prophet's vision in a valley of dry bones, he preached a message full of hope; and he prayed. Then "the breath came into them, and they lived, and stood up upon their feet, an exceedingly great army" (Ezek. 37:10). According to the New Testament such a transforming experience comes to believers one at a time.

A message about "The Birth from Above" may lead to one about prayer. In the apostolic Church the Spirit bade a humble believer do personal work with Saul of Tarsus, the

Church's Public Enemy Number One. When the believer held back, the Spirit gave this assurance about Saul: "Behold, he prayeth" (Acts 9:11d). Saul had often said his prayers; at last he knelt down and prayed. A still better text comes from the Gospel that tells most about prayer: "As he was praying in a certain place, . . . one of his disciples said unto him, Lord, teach us to pray" (Luke 11:1). These words led George Adam Smith, a brilliant Old Testament expositor, to preach about "The Lord's Example in Prayer":

  I. Our Lord bases prayer on God's fatherhood.
 II. Christ looks on prayer as life's battlefield.
III. He finds in prayer a new inspiration for service.

What a way to preach about prayer—the Christian meaning of prayer! In making ready for the sermon, the professor studied his passage with care. He must also have had an "illuminating flash." Think of prayer as "life's battlefield"! What a vista for a sermon! Especially near the end the message is shot through with still other light. The preacher shows that prayer ought to lift a person above the clouds of earth. He says that one day in the Alps he kept toiling up a steep ascent, under the care of two guides, one going before and the other coming after. At last, breathless, the three men drew near the summit, which consisted of splintered rocks protruding from the snow. The leader stepped aside to let the stranger behold the glories of earth and sky. Seeing that the young man was about to stand erect, the second guide dragged him back and exclaimed: "On your knees, sir, on your knees, on your knees! You are never safe here except on your knees!" [4]

⁴ *Forgiveness of Sins* (New York: Eaton & Mains, 1905), pp. 69-88.

CHAPTER ELEVEN

THE MATERIAL
FROM RELATED READINGS

R EADING MAKETH A FULL MAN," SAID FRANCIS BACON. Full of what—wisdom or wind? That depends on what one reads, whether truth or tripe; and on how, with a system or a sieve. In addition to books on the Bible one should "read, mark, learn, and inwardly digest" works of theology, so as to have a growing knowledge of the best that has been written. Every pastor needs to become his own librarian. Visitors from abroad report that an American minister likely has a first-class automobile and a fourth-class library.

READING BOOKS ABOUT DOCTRINE

A library should include books about the Cross. This trail would lead to the Early Fathers, but we shall consider only the books of modern authors. As for "manuals," "digests," and "compendia," they have their uses, but not for an educated minister. He goes to the sources from which compilers draw. James Reid, for example, preached on the text "Behold the Lamb of God, which taketh away the sin of the world" (John 1:29). Without quoting or seeming bookish, he showed a working knowledge of the literature. He was preaching, not parading scholarship or parroting sources:

This word is John's contribution towards the solution of the biggest problem in history—the personality of Jesus Christ. . . . We do not see Christ clearly till we see Him in relation to sin. It was sin that slew Jesus Christ. . . . Our salvation does not depend upon our theory of the Atonement. It depends on our experience of Christ's love. . . . Every view of the Cross of Christ—and there have been many views of it—is just man's feeble attempt to put into words what Christ put into the Cross, the love of God which passeth knowledge. . . . If you do not see that, you miss the heart of the Gospel.[1]

Reid tells of a former soldier with only one arm. A stranger said to him: "Old man, I see that the war has taken it out of you." Glancing down at his sleeve without an arm, the veteran replied: "Oh, no, I gave it!" The sermon does not consist of stories. It gives three answers to the question "How does the death of Christ take away sin?"

The Cross
  I. Awakens men to the reality and consciousness of sin.
 II. Reveals God's love and forgiveness, making them ours.
III. Leads to full deliverance, which sets us free.

All true, but still the mystery remains!

This man digested his books and knew his facts. He used materials as a quarterback in football uses successive plays to advance the ball. Such an idea of preaching calls for the exclusion of everything that would retard progress or distract attention. Other men have preached this way, because of reading. For a while we may think about titles of books from which they have drawn knowledge and inspiration.

PREACHING ABOUT THE CROSS

Before Easter have a number of sermons on *The Cross in Christian Experience* (W. M. Clow). Some subjects that follow may call for sermons beyond the reach of churches

[1] *The Victory of God* (London: Hodder & Stoughton, Ltd., 1933), pp. 47-57. Used by permission of the author and publisher.

not accustomed to such preaching, but a man can learn to translate any idea into terms clear to a layman. According to the late Lord Rutherford, foremost physicist of yesterday, no scientific discovery can be counted complete "until it has been described in simple and correct language." The same holds true in theology.

By way of background think of *Sacrifice in the Old Testament* (G. B. Gray). If the subject seems vast and remote from local needs, turn to *The Cross of Hosea* (H. W. Robinson), a truth that calls for tears. Later, *The Atonement in New Testament Teaching* (Vincent Taylor). "I delivered unto you first of all that which I also received, how that Christ died for our sins according to the scriptures" (I Cor. 15:3). In such a message somehow limit the field. Few hearers can follow sweeping surveys that delight ministers. In a sermon about the Cross a layman ought to learn one large truth that he will remember as long as he lives.

Once a brilliant interpreter spoke to students of divinity about the "hidden wisdom" of the Cross. As an eloquent advocate of "New Theology," R. J. Campbell had earlier preached about other things good; but as he grew older, he found delight in truths that centered in the Cross. So he pleaded with young ministers to preach the Gospel. What follows refers to the preaching of Paul. It appears now because it shows that a man of ability can present the Gospel in a form too condensed for lay hearers not versed in such lore:

His Gospel is that of the Saviour who died that we might live, of a forgiveness made possible by a divine sacrifice, of a righteousness not our own, to be appropriated by faith, of a joyful sharing in the life of the risen and exalted Lord, of final victory over sin and death. . . . The cardinal error of the Church today is that we talk as though we believed that men could be saved in the mass, instead of one by one.[2]

That preacher had read much and thought much. In the light of personal experience he had worked out his own way of looking at things, only to find that he had come back to the teachings of Paul. Like Oliver Wendell Holmes, when asked about what he read before he wrote, Campbell might have replied: "I have milked three hundred cows, but I make my own butter." The same would apply to the author of *God Was in Christ* (D. M. Baillie). The title points to a Bible chapter where Paul most strongly presents his interpretation of the Cross, especially in this verse: "God was in Christ, reconciling the world unto himself" (II Cor. 5:19). This chapter earlier led to *The Christian Doctrine of Reconciliation* (James Denney).

Preaching about the Cross in terms of reconciliation accords with the thinking of many laymen. Reconciliation means God's way of bringing us into right relations with Himself, against whom we have sinned, "most grievously." If we wished to complicate the picture, we might insist, with some scholars, that God Himself needed to be reconciled. In the passage at hand and in the resulting sermon, God stands as the supreme Reconciler. I mean God in Christ through the Holy Spirit, as revealed in Scripture and confirmed in Christian experience. All this a man ought to believe and preach, but not in one sermon or in two, lest the bewildered layman become still more confused.

Before a man preaches much on reconciliation, he ought to read such books as the above, with an older one by a

[2] *Vision and Life* (New York: The Macmillan Co., 1929), p. 65.

141

German liberal, *Justification and Reconciliation* (Albrecht Ritschl). The sermon ought to make clear that the supreme Reconciler has done all He can do for us sinners. He has loved us with everlasting love, and He has never made light of our sins. He hates them vastly more than a young mother hates poliomyelitis when it strikes her first-born child. God is not at peace with sin, and never can be at peace with it, until it is done to death. This He has wrought through the Cross, to bring us into the household of the redeemed and set us free to serve.

Without making light of the second Person in the Trinity, preach on the primacy of the Father in the work of redemption. Many churchgoers feel that the Lord Jesus is on our side and that the Father is against us or else neutral. In a home that I once knew well, a girl of five told her mother: "I love Jesus, but I don't love God."

"Mary, that's awful! What do you mean?"

"Mama, Jesus paid it all; God didn't do a thing!"

Instead of spanking the child for echoing what she had learned in Bible school, the mother asked me what to tell Mary. I did not know, but I found out. Later I preached on the subject, with no reference to Mary and her mother.

The doctrine of God's primacy does not rest on proof texts. Still it helped me to make a list of golden texts about redemption. On one side I put those that ascribe salvation to God the Father; on the other side, those that do not. Without making an exhaustive study I found that the majority of my favorite texts ascribe salvation primarily to God the Father. "God so loved . . . that he gave" (John 3:16). "Herein is love, not that we loved God, but that he loved us" (I John 4:10). "God commendeth his love toward us" (Rom. 5:8). "God hath not appointed us to wrath, but to obtain salvation" (I Thess. 5:9). In these texts, as in others, God shows His love through the Cross of Christ.

Another term, "Atonement," calls for interpretation, which comes through a British work, *The Way of At-One-Ment* (W. J. Phythian-Adams). Here too the stress falls on the will of God and on the Cross of Christ. In Ephesians, for example, the first chapter glories in what the Father has done for our redemption. The second shows what Christ has done on the Cross: "He is our peace, who hath made both one, and hath broken down the middle wall of partition" (vs. 14). The third chapter shows what a minister like Paul can do by preaching and prayer. The remaining three chapters make clear how we ought to live because we have been redeemed. Thank God for His At-one-ment!

A more difficult term, "ransom," has come to the fore because of an able book, *Christus Victor* (Gustaf Aulén). Some of us used to look askance at the ransom theory. From Aulén we have learned that it means as much now as in the early Church, where it prevailed. We now see this doctrine in the key verse of the Second Gospel: "The Son of man came not to be ministered unto, but to minister, and to give his life a ransom" (10:45). When Christ uttered these words, He was drawing near to *The Day of the Cross* (W. M. Clow). In *The Training of the Twelve* (A. B. Bruce), He rebuked self-seeking young ministers and pointed to the Cross as our supreme example of the greatness that consists in service. A "life-situation sermon"!

LIKENESS TO CHRIST ON THE CROSS

I. Christ came from heaven to save us from sin.
II. On the Cross He paid the cost of our freedom.
III. To be a Christian means to be like Him on the Cross.

Through His death Christ redeemed. In this respect we can never resemble Him, but we can become like Him in His desire to serve at any cost. As for the cost to Him, why not preach directly about the ransom? Some of us hesitate because of an old classroom question that we cannot answer: To whom did He pay the ransom? Learned men of yesterday, such as James Orr, of Glasgow, could say without batting an eye: "He paid the ransom to God." That put God in a queer light. Other solons insisted: "Christ paid the ransom to Satan." That "solution" raised more dust than it settled. Personally, I do not know to whom Christ paid the ransom, and I do not care. In the Scriptures I find neither the question nor the answer.

I never heard a layman raise this question, but I have known hosts of laymen who rejoiced in what we call the ransom theory. They got it from old-time songs about being set free from a bondage worse than that of Hebrew serfs in Egypt under Pharaoh. Beginning with Negro spirituals based on Exodus, any lover of Christian doctrine set to music can make a collection of songs about being

> Loosed from Pharaoh's bitter yoke,
> Israel's sons and daughters.

In a fourteenth-century hymn two stanzas close with echoes of the ransom theory:

> Who did once, upon the cross, Alleluia!
> Suffer to redeem our loss. Alleluia!
>
> .   .   .   .
>
> Who endured the cross and grave, Alleluia!
> Sinners to redeem and save. Alleluia!

A case from history throws light on our classroom question. At Rome in the days of Flavius Honorius as emperor, the populace used to assemble in a vast amphitheater to witness gladiatorial combats. Intent on putting an end to the slaughter of men made in the image of God, a monk named Telemachus went from Asia Minor to Rome, more than one thousand miles. Having failed in every other way, one day he ran down into the arena and pleaded with the combatants not to slay one another. Infuriated by this interference with their sport, the people swarmed down onto the field and beat the monk to death. Then the emperor issued an edict forbidding gladiatorial combats.

That monk gave his life. To whom did he give it? I do not know, but I know that his deed stirs my heart. I think of myself when young. What if I had been a captive in a Roman dungeon, awaiting a call into the arena, there to slay or be slain? All at once there had come tidings that I might go free, because a good man had died. On the way home to my wife and little ones I might have wept with gratitude for what he had done. I should never have dreamed of asking: "To whom did he pay the ransom?"

APPEALING TO MEN'S HEARTS

The pulpit should give a worthy place to "the theology of the feelings." Paul and John did so. Neither of them ever looked on the glories of redemption as matters for cold, scientific research. Philosophic speculations have their place, but not when a man speaks to sinners about their Saviour. A minister never has time enough to answer all the questions men keep asking or ought to be asking. They want answers from the heart, even more than the head. With some such homemade screen a pastor can keep out of his sermons many questions as troublesome as mosquitoes.

Men's hearts respond to a sermon about *The Healing Cross*

145

(H. H. Farmer). This points to our Lord as the divine Physician, a figure that one ought not to carry further than the Scriptures warrant. Like Philip the evangelist, one can preach from the old-time words "With his stripes we are healed" (Isa. 53:5). Here the fact means far more than the figure. The fact points to Christ. In dealing with a stranger from Ethiopia, Philip began at this same scripture and preached unto him Jesus (Acts 8:35).

The meaning of the figure appears in a book, *The Disease and Remedy of Sin* (W. M. Mackay). While not brilliant in style, or up to the minute in psychology, this volume points out many ways to preach on Christianity and sin in terms of spiritual health and disease. Such sermons appeal to laymen in an era when everybody feels concerned about health and disease. See *The Sickness unto Death* by Soren Kierkegaard.

"The Healing Power of the Cross" (John 3:14-15) bids men:
I. Look on sin as the deadliest disease.
II. Find in the Cross the way to be cured.
III. Show gratitude to God by engaging in service.

Many a person does not feel grateful for anything good. During World War II a young captain on a battlefield saw that a sergeant had been seriously wounded. Knowing that he risked his life, the captain ran out and dragged the sergeant to safety. Then the captain fell down and died from his wounds. In time the sergeant recovered, and after the war he went home. One night he was entertained as guest of honor in the home of the captain's parents. Arriving late, half intoxicated, the sergeant acted like a boor. After a bountiful meal, which he wolfed down, he hastened away with never a word about the man who had died in his stead. Then the mother of the captain burst into sobs and exclaimed to her husband: "To think that our son had to die for a thing like that!"

The Voice from the Cross (A. W. Blackwood, Jr.) and *The Inward Cross* (C. D. Kean) serve as titles of books about the Seven Last Words. The latter phrase would go with Paul's words about "The Cross in the Heart": "I am crucified with Christ" (Gal. 2:20). In appealing to hardhearted Galatians the Apostle relied largely on his own experience of transforming grace.

All the theologies that have ever been framed have been just so many efforts to express what the humblest servant of Christ knows in his heart; namely, that in a sinful world it is inevitable that by the Cross the Saviour should enter into His glory, and that those who have entered most fully into the fellowship of the Cross have been conscious that it contains the clue to the mystery of earthly existence as a whole.

These preaching "leads" have come from titles of books about the Cross. While unequal in value, they all seem to me worth reading. Other works, second to none in value, bear titles that do not interpret: for example, *The Death of Christ* (James Denney) and *The Nature of the Atonement* (J. M. Campbell). Anyone who knows the field can add other titles. If I were a pastor, I should not go far through a book of theology unless I could find in it something to preach, after making it my own.

QUOTING WHAT ONE READS

A pastor who reads should beware lest he quote too much. Until recently, in the history of preaching the ablest men seldom quoted, except from the Bible. F. W. Robertson, for instance, ranged widely through world literature. He knew almost by heart Dante's *Inferno*, much of it in the Italian, said to be difficult. Robertson's sermons contained few quotations or scholarly allusions. The same held true of Brooks and many another pulpit master who reveled in volumes the world counted great.

Today the fashion seems to have changed. Our ablest men quote as freely now as second-raters used to do. With George A. Buttrick, Paul E. Scherer, Ralph W. Sockman, the Luccocks, father and son, and others, the custom seems to justify itself. Among their imitators "quotitis" raises serious questions. Men who quote effectively know the sources firsthand and use them with culture and restraint. Without some such background quoters of borrowed material may turn out sermons consisting of shreds and patches, like a crazy quilt.

A first-class book, *The Mystery of Preaching*, by James Black,[3] warns against quoting. Paradoxically, the author relies on quotations, which I borrow. "Have you ever noticed," asked James Denney, "that the Apostles seldom quote, except from the source of their authority?" "In my experience of listening to sermons," declared George Adam Smith, "no art is more difficult than that of using relevant quotations." The following comes to me from John Oman: "Preach with authority, not with authorities." Christ "taught as one having authority, and not as the scribes" (Matt. 7:29). This next comes from Howard Thurman: "Why do you quote so many authorities in your new book? If what you are saying is true, you do not need the authorities. If what you are saying is not true, all the authorities in the world cannot make it true."

A kindred question relates to borrowing from printed ser-

[3] Pp. 127-28.

mons. Many of us believe in reading sermons, if worthy, much as a professional painter likes to study the work of master artists. If a reader of sermons borrows a topic occasionally, that can do no harm unless he does it surreptitiously. As for taking over a sermon *in toto*, scooping it up with a shovel, that lessens a man's self-respect and may interfere with his usefulness. Any graduate of Princeton University knows that plagiarism, if detected, leads to expulsion. When he reads a sermon that his pastor has filched, and used without giving credit, the layman wonders if the parson knows the meaning of the commandment "Thou shalt not steal." In all such cases a self-made rule will help: If in doubt, don't!

Guidance here comes from Bernard of Clairvaux, prince of preachers. His eighty-six sermons on the first two chapters of the Canticles show how not to preach from the Bible. These allegorical messages about the incarnate Lord get as far from the Bible passages as East is from West. Nevertheless, Bernard has much to say, and he often says it memorably. In the eighteenth sermon he begins with a text full of quiet beauty: "Thy name is as ointment poured forth" (Song of S. 1:3*b*). The excerpt that follows sets up an ideal for every preacher of doctrine today:

If . . . you are wise, you will show yourself rather as a reservoir than as a canal. For a canal spreads abroad water as it receives it, but a reservoir waits until it is filled before overflowing, and thus communicates, without loss to itself, its superabundant water. . . . In the Church at the present day we have many canals, few reservoirs.[4]

---

[4] *Cantica Canticorum*, tr. Samuel J. Eales (London: Elliot Stock, 1895).

CHAPTER TWELVE

THE IMPORTANCE
OF A TEACHING TOPIC

I N A DOCTRINAL SERMON THE TOPIC SEEMS MORE important than in other kinds of pulpit work. The preacher of a doctrinal message wishes the layman to remember the subject as the gist of all he has heard. A. J. Gossip once preached on "The Meaning of Infant Baptism" (Mark 9:36). After a single reading of the sermon I could easily recall his subject, but not his passage. I still remember what he stressed, but not what he passed over lightly. These ideas about a preacher's aim and a hearer's memory permit all sorts of exceptions. Still it can never do any harm to give a doctrinal sermon a teaching topic that the hearer can remember with ease.

A topic means the name of a sermon. A teaching topic means that the wording of the subject shows what the layman should learn. The subject of an inspirational sermon does not try to teach. In the same volume as above, *Experience Worketh Hope*, Gossip has an inspiring message: "The Day Dreams of a Christian Man" (Phil. 3:20). What does that mean? The topic merely suggests the answer that comes out in the sermon. This sermon is topical, by which I mean that the sermon develops and discusses the subject with which it starts. The word "topical" bears no stigma and no sting. Indeed, it may be a badge of honor.

Other men employ the word "topic" differently. Nobody can use such labels with scientific accuracy, as in dealing with poisonous drugs. In the preface of a book, *That Immortal*

Sea (1953), Leslie D. Weatherhead wrote: "I have not included any topical sermons." He may have meant no treatments of secular subjects, especially if sensational. Whatever he meant, he had a right to use the word his way. All but three of his seventeen sermons seem to me topical. The book closes with one about "The Last of Life," from Browning's "Rabbi Ben Ezra": "The last of life, for which the first was made." With a stanza of this poem the sermon begins, and then goes on, in the way of good topical sermons.

LEARNING FROM PULPIT MASTERS

In the history of preaching, says Clarence E. Macartney, every sermon of the first rank has been topical. He preaches this way, but without secular content. In the English-speaking world three sermons have become known as "greatest." All three are doctrinal, at least indirectly; and all three are topical. In the best of the three Horace Bushnell begins with a topic: "Every Man's Life a Plan of God" (Isa. 45:5). In the second Brooks makes everything center around his topic: "The Fire and the Calf" (Exod. 32:24). In the third James B. Mozley stresses a topic: "The Reversal of Human Judgments" (Matt. 19:30).

If I were to add a fourth, it would be the sermon by Gossip "But When Life Tumbles in, What Then?" (Jer. 12:5). Indirectly doctrinal and decidedly topical! As a lover of expository work I can think of only one such sermon that has become famous, and that by a layman: "The Greatest Thing in the World" (I Cor. 13:13) by Henry Drummond. Like most first-class expository work, this message owes much to its topic. Whatever the label, the idea is that a first-class subject helps the layman to remember the gist of what he has heard. If so, the seed has fallen into good soil.

Some topics make no such impression, popularly. In 1918 P. T. Forsyth sent out a little book with an appealing title: *This Life and the Next.*[1] Whenever he so desired, Forsyth could coin phrases with telling effect. He says that when we talk about the life to come, we usually mean "a second cycle of this one, better oiled." He insists that Christ must become either the occupant of a man's heart or else a bystander. On the other hand, some of his chapter headings show how not to name popular sermons: "The Egoism of Immortality," "The Egoism of God," "The Fructification of Failure," "*De Mortuis*," and "*L'Envoi.*"

In that same year Robert Law, of Toronto, sent out a volume, *The Hope of Our Calling.* Without the brilliance and depth of Forsyth, this man knew how to prepare doctrinal sermons for laymen. Addressing people who knew the Bible, he spoke about "The Hereafter in the Old Testament" (Job 14:14). Again, "Death, Blessing or Curse?" (I Cor. 15: 56). In true biblical fashion the blessing precedes the curse, as sunshine comes before shadow. Nothing thrilling here, but much to attract attention and satisfy the soul.

PREACHING ON THE RESURRECTION

In preaching on "The Resurrection of Christ," Law states his purpose. He does not plan to deal with the credibility of the Resurrection, but to exhibit its meaning. "To anyone who may be in difficulty let me say from my own experience that the first step towards assurance of its reliability is to understand its meaning." Only in passing does he try to show the validity of the doctrine. The sermon proper consists of three parts:

[1] New York: The Macmillan Co., 1918.

The Resurrection of Christ is:

I. The one positive and tangible proof of life beyond.
II. The guarantee of personal identity after death.
III. The guarantee of victory for the divine life.

This last part includes an illustration:

When Columbus was seeking for the New World he saw one day strange birds flying overhead, and pieces of vegetation floating on the waves, which he perceived were natives not of the sea but of the land, and knew that he was drawing near to the end of his quest. But no sign ever comes to us from that [unseen] world, no flotsam from its shores. . . . Not one of those who have gone before us, of those we have known and loved, has come back to tell us what is there. But now our Columbus has sailed back from the New World. He has "brought life and immortality to light." [2]

As Christians we should think more about resurrection than about immortality. At one time I questioned the idea of resurrection. Like many other college men I believed in the survival of the soul and felt little concern about the future of the body. Later I found that the New Testament assumes the fact of immortality and stresses the fact of resurrection. Since our Lord died only in His body, His Resurrection must have concerned only His body. The same holds true of His followers. If I did not believe in the future existence of spiritual bodies, I could not say in the Creed: "I believe in . . . the resurrection of the body." Other men whom I honor state these facts differently. We all ought to search the Scriptures and accept what they teach.

[2] (New York: George H. Doran Co., 1918.) Used by permission of McClelland and Stewart, Ltd.

In a little book, *The Resurrection and the Life*, Weatherhead has five chapters with headings worthy of note. They would serve as the topics in a series of sermons:

I. Christ Is Risen.
II. Christ Is Alive Today.
III. Christ Offers Life Now.
IV. Christ Offers Life Hereafter.
V. Christ Is Relevant to Life Today.

Though topical in form, these messages are Christ-centered and contemporary. An excerpt shows the bearing on everyday life:

A girl was converted in my former church in Leeds, and after some months she came back to my room after a service and said, "It's no good. Religion doesn't work. I'm just as bad-tempered as ever. I'm giving it up."

I won't bore you with what I said to her. . . . She had not been gone ten minutes when her father, who did not know she had been to church that evening, came in and put down a generous donation on the table for the work of my Men's Samaritan League among the poor. I said, "What's this for?"

"I'm giving you that," he said, "because since my daughter started coming here, she's not only a different girl, but my home's a different place. The whole atmosphere's different." [3]

What has this to do with naming a doctrinal sermon? Much, every way! In preparing such a message one puts into the topic the gist of what one plans to say. In the sermon from beginning to end one keeps discussing the subject with which one starts. In days to come the hearer will recall the topic, at least in substance, and follow it as a beacon light in daily living. But not unless the friend "in the minister's workshop"

[3] (New York and Nashville: Abingdon Press, 1949), p. 23. Used by permission of the publisher.

knows how to set up a beacon light and how to "follow the beam."

A doctrinal preacher may never announce a subject in advance. Even so, he can use a topic as a guide in gathering and sifting material, and in preparing the sermon, both as a whole and in every part. At Easter he may single out the words: "Now is Christ risen from the dead, and become the firstfruits of them that slept" (I Cor. 15:20). After a study of the passage in its setting, he decides to preach about "Easter in Terms of Harvest." He thinks of the Holy Land, where barley harvest comes about Easter and is the happiest season of the year. In olden days a farmer brought to the sanctuary the first sheaf of ripe grain as a token that the harvest had come from God and was to be used for His glory. The sermon may consist of two large truths:

I. Christ's Resurrection: beginning the heavenly harvest
II. Our resurrection: completing the heavenly harvest

The idea of harvest should dominate the sermon. The opening sentence, the rest of a brief introduction, the main headings, the key sentences of the successive paragraphs, the few illustrations, and the conclusion—all ought to sound the same motif. If the figure was not full of interest, and if the fact did not tell of future joy, iteration might become boresome. Not if the minister has visited the Holy Land at harvest time, or if he can read the Scriptures with a seeing eye.

AVOIDING ANY CAMOUFLAGE

In naming a doctrinal sermon avoid camouflage. In other sorts of preaching, if you wish to inspire but not inform, start with a topic that does not teach. For instance, take Gossip's subject: "How Spring Comes to the Soul" (John 11:25-26).

Such pulpit work calls for a seeing eye and an artist's taste. Otherwise the desire to attract may lead to such a subject as "God's Garage." Text: "I go to prepare a place for you" (John 14:2). Even if the topic were in keeping with the text, what about good taste? Why ask the hearer to think of heaven in terms of a messy garage? For many reasons a doctrinal preacher should never stoop to "smartness" in sermon subjects. They may smell of a garage.

Neither should a teaching minister resort to camouflage. If he wishes to preach on the Deity of Christ, let him say so, and tie up the truth with something about the hearers: "The Deity of Christ: The Difference to Us." Text: the key verse of the Fourth Gospel (20:31). The sermon may have two parts, in common with both text and topic:

I. The Fourth Gospel was written to teach the Deity of Christ.
II. The doctrine of His Deity insures our salvation.

Deity here means in part that we worship Christ as we worship no one but God. To Christ we sing praises in church. To Him we pray, as Stephen did when dying (Acts 7:59-60). In Christ's name, with that of the Father and the Spirit, the minister baptizes converts and pronounces the benediction. So much for the meaning. What of the difference to us? Because of Christ's Deity we know that He has power and authority to save and rule, to comfort and bless.

> No mortal can with Him compare
> Among the sons of men.

The hearer will not remember the entire sermon; but he should never forget the two words that keep ringing out: Deity and difference. The Deity has to do with doctrine about Him. The difference relates to duty for us. Believe and live! As a young pastor I used to preach some such sermon, with no camouflage, once every winter, usually at night. One Monday morning I met on the street a lawyer of early middle age. In thanking me for the sermon the night before, he referred to the topic. Then he gave me the best lecture I had ever heard about what to preach:

We laymen get fed up with pretty sermonettes about the beauty of leaves and birds. We want to hear about God and men, sin and salvation, heaven and hell. We wish to know what to believe about Christ's Deity, and what difference it makes to us on Main Street. It helps a man like me to keep straight and clean from Monday morning through Saturday night when he feels sure of Christ as the Son of God.

Not every young minister feels ready for forthright doctrinal preaching. For example,

If one takes the writings of Lloyd Douglas as a declaration of his beliefs over the years, one can trace a gradual change in his viewpoint concerning the divinity of Christ. . . . In his early novels any contacts with a divine experience appear mysterious and dream-like. In *The Robe* the hero Marcellus is described as being a skeptic until late in the book, when he says, "I believe." But in *The Big Fisherman* Christ is depicted as a divine figure at all times. . . . It would seem as if the author himself at last believed.[4]

Parts of this excerpt show the mental state of many laymen now. They revere the Lord Jesus, but need to know more about Him. Partly for this reason some of them become Roman Catholics. An intelligent woman had been reared a Roman Catholic, but after a mixed marriage she became a

[4] V. D. Dawson and B. D. Wilson, *The Shape of Sunday: An Intimate Biography of Lloyd C. Douglas* (by his daughters) (Boston: Houghton Mifflin Co., 1952), p. 369. Used by permission of the publisher.

"practicing Presbyterian." She told me that she noticed a striking difference between the two churches: Roman Catholics stressed the Deity of Christ; Presbyterians, the humanity. She would have welcomed a clear, kind message without camouflage, such as: "Why Protestants Worship Christ." Better still: "Why We Believe in Christ's Deity." That might call for something about the word "Deus," which means God, and about the ancient chant *Te Deum Laudamus*, especially this part:

> Thou art the King of Glory: O Christ.
> Thou art the everlasting Son: of the Father.
>
> . . . .
>
> O Lord, save Thy people: and bless Thine heritage.

NAMING YOUR BRAIN CHILD

A resourceful preacher has sermons informative and sermons inspirational, with two different sorts of names. The two kinds of brain children should differ as a little boy differs from a wee girl. Think of an informative message as calling for a subject with strength and energy, of an inspirational sermon as calling for a topic with grace and charm. If a minister prepares both sorts of sermons, and gives each of them a name that fits, his people will never complain that all his pulpit work seems alike. Sometimes he will have solid food, well cooked and served warm. At other times he will prepare for "sweetness and light," as at a marriage feast.

Discarding the figure, let us think about ten principles, not on a par with the Ten Commandments. Also ten working rules, binding only when they fit the facts in the case.

I. *Importance.* Homiletically, in a doctrinal sermon nothing save the text seems to me so important as the topic. It should dominate everything.

II. *Religion.* Since a teaching topic tells the truth, it ought to be religious. If not, either the message is secular or the name is a misnomer.

III. *Purpose.* A sermon directly doctrinal calls for a topic that shows the purpose. An inspirational topic may conceal where a teaching subject should reveal.

IV. *Clarity.* In a teaching sermon, as in a teaching book, the name should be clear. If not, how can it teach?

V. *Honesty.* A preacher's word should be as good as his bond. With a teaching topic he should do what he promises. Why seem to gain a hearing under false pretenses?

VI. *Interest.* Any doctrinal subject bearing on human needs today proves interesting, but only if well phrased. Make it glow!

VII. *Sensationalism.* Since World War II few men have searched the gutter for sermon subjects. But many topics seem as stale as last week's toast.

VIII. *Phrasing.* The desired phrasing may come to mind early, but the final decision should come after the brain child has been born. On Monday a man can seldom know exactly what he will preach on Sunday, but he should know the substance.

IX. *Length.* A topic that teaches may run longer than one that inspires. As in a newspaper ad, a careful craftsman uses no more than four big words.

X. *Variety.* Except in a series, plan for variety from week to week; also from morning to evening. This may prove to be the hardest of all the suggestions, and the most important. As to how, see the ten "rules" that follow:

1. *Parallelism.* In a series the subjects follow much the same pattern. As with quintuplets, all girls, likeness of character calls for similarity of names.

2. *A Noun and a Phrase*. The most common sort of topic, which some of us use too often: "The Resurrection in Our Street" (I Cor. 15:58).

3. *A Question*. Direct: "Why Must a Good Man Suffer?" (Job 1:8). Indirect: "How God Answers Prayer" (Luke 11:13). Never raise a question about what the Bible assumes to be true: "Is There a God"? (Ps. 14:1a).

4. *A Heading and a Question*. "The Resurrection of the Body: What Does It Mean?" (I Cor. 15:38). Too long for a bulletin board.

5. *A Question and an Answer*. James S. Stewart: "Who Is This Jesus?" (I) "Behold the Man!" (II) "Behold Your God!" The topics of two sermons in succession.

6. *A Double Topic*. "The Atonement and the Modern Mind." Often used. Not always accurate. The two parts unequal in value.

7. *Direct Address*. "Let the Church Be the Church" (E. G. Homrighausen). In skillful hands, effective. Otherwise, irritating.

8. *A Declarative Sentence*. "A New Jerusalem We Seek" (Timothy T. Lew, a Christian poet). When well done, occasionally admirable.

9. *A Part of the Text*. Among two hundred printed sermons by Brooks about a third quote or echo the text. "Going Up to Jerusalem" (Luke 18:30). Good at times. As a rule the topic should interpret the text, especially in preaching doctrine.

10. *A Borrowed Subject*. Ordinarily a minister phrases his own topics. If he borrows occasionally, the heavens will not fall. In each case the Spirit will guide.

CHAPTER THIRTEEN

THE NECESSITY
OF STURDY STRUCTURE

DOCTRINAL PREACHING, IF DIRECT, CALLS FOR sturdy structure which stands out. The discussion follows a plan, with stages clearly visible. If a sermon is to teach, it should have unity, order, progress, and climax. A message chiefly inspirational pays less attention to structure, except the climax. Every sermon, like every novel, needs a basic plan; but the profusion of the vine may conceal the shape of the trellis. For example, take the well-known sermon by Gossip "But When Life Tumbles in, What Then?"

At first this message seems to have no structure. The sermon seems to consist in a torrential succession of mighty words, rushing along like the Jordan overflowing its banks. On closer study the sermon reveals a careful plan. It all has to do with God's providence amid life's disasters. The sermon proper has two main parts, each of which takes 121 lines. Structure mighty as steel, but all out of sight! How inspiring!

DECIDING ON A BASIC PATTERN

Let us think about a sermon directly doctrinal, with sturdy structure. Once at Princeton a graduate student from Czechoslovakia asked what I meant by this term. Knowing that he revered our visiting professor, and thought well of his daughter, I answered: "Dr. Hromadka has sturdy structure, with wide-spreading shoulders. His daughter has nothing of the sort; she has sylphlike grace and charm."

In preparing for a doctrinal sermon a man needs an overall pattern. A "sermon builder" may settle on a plan too soon. Before he sees the objective, studies the terrain, and knows the available materials, he decides about the spans for a bridge. He may have used the same plan for the last bridge, and he may do so with the next one. "Skeletons," exclaimed Spurgeon about sermon plans by students at his Pastor's College. "Skeletons without the Holy Ghost!" He wanted every sermon to have a bony framework, but always inside a living body.

Guidance here comes from Henry van Dyke. As a master of living prose, a professor of English, and a preacher of note, he studied the way a man's mind works before he can write a piece of literature. Van Dyke says that four elements enter into what I call the making of a plan. The fourth refers also to literary style, but that does not concern us in this chapter.

An original impulse—not necessarily a new idea, but a new sense of the value of an idea.

A first hand study of the subject and the material.

A patient, joyful, unsparing labor for the perfection of form.

A human aim—to cheer, console, purify or ennoble the life of the people. Without this aim literature has never sent an arrow close to the mark.

One may start with a mental pattern already made, but one should keep the matter open. After a period of study and "subconscious incubation," one may shift to another design, still more simple. Mark Twain once wrote to van Dyke about the difficulty of finding the right plan for a short story, perhaps the length of a sermon:

It costs me as many false starts [for a short story as a long one. And] the right start—the right *plan*—is the only difficulty encountered. . . . I have hardly ever started a story, long or short, on the right plan—the right plan being the plan which will make it tell itself without my help—except after three failures. . . . Only the born artist can expect to start a story right the first time.[1]

Not being a born artist, a doctrinal preacher usually has to work hard and think much before he sees the right plan. The effectiveness of the sermon will depend on what comes first, what follows next, in stage after stage, climactically, and what comes last, persuasively. All this a minister ought to see before he makes a final plan and starts to write. When once clearly in view, the right plan leads to its own unfolding, but only if the maker has collected the necessary materials.

INTRODUCING THE HOLY SPIRIT

A pastor may feel a "new impulse" to preach about the Holy Spirit. He wishes to introduce the Spirit to people who know little about Him except His name. Not seeing how to approach the difficult subject, the minister starts to read the book of the Acts. Then he may turn to *The Christian Experience of the Holy Spirit* by H. Wheeler Robinson.[2] The attitude of the author appears in this part of the Introduction:

In the course of a serious illness [the writer] was led to ask himself why the truths of "evangelical" Christianity which he had often preached to others now failed to bring him personal strength. They remained true to him, but they seemed to lack vitality. . . . The result of this experience was . . . to lead him to seek for the lacuna in his own conception of evangelical truth. He found it in his relative neglect of those conceptions of the Holy Spirit in which the New Testament is so rich.

A pastor who has had no such experience may need to have

[1] Tertius van Dyke, *Henry van Dyke* (New York: Harper & Bros., 1935), pp. 203, 218. Used by permission of the publisher.

[2] (London: Nisbet & Co., 1932), p. 4.

one. As soon as his heart begins to burn with a new discovery of the Holy Spirit, he can make ready to share the
vision with his people. In "the most exciting book of the
New Testament" he may preach from the key verse: "Ye
shall receive power, after that the Holy Ghost is come upon
you" (Acts 1:8). "The Power of God in Our Church." The
opening sentences may deal with the need for power, locally.
The sermon headings may come in the form of alliteration.
If unforced and true to the facts, alliteration helps, but not
as a regular diet. According to the text in its setting, the Holy
Spirit in the life of a church means power that is personal—
present—practical—available through prayer.

The Holy Spirit also means the wisdom of God. "When
he, the Spirit of truth, is come, he will guide you into all
truth" (John 16:33). Churchgoers need to know what to
believe, how to live, and what to hope for. All this they can
learn, one truth at a time, if they read the Bible under the
guidance of the Holy Spirit. For an example turn to an able
biography, *Booker T. Washington: Educator and Interracial
Interpreter*.[3] At his home in Tuskegee the schoolman kept in
every room a copy of the Bible. Whenever he had a few minutes free, he would take up a Bible and read a portion in
the spirit of prayer. According to his daughter "he read the
Bible to us at breakfast every day, and prayed. Really he
prayed all the time."

MAKING A SERMON PRACTICAL

Booker T. Washington faced a lifework like that of Moses
in leading his people out of bondage. Many a leader now desires such an experience as Phillips Brooks presents: "O, do

[3] By Basil Mathews (Cambridge, Mass.: Harvard University Press, 1948),
pp. 161, 190.

not pray for easy lives. Pray to be stronger men! Do not pray for tasks equal to your powers. Pray for powers equal to [your] tasks!"[4] Alas for the leader who does not know where to look! As a man of science, not a Christian, Thomas Huxley once wrote, wistfully: "If some great Power would agree to make me always think what is true and do what is right, on condition of being turned into a sort of clock, and wound up every morning, I should instantly close with the offer."[5] If Huxley had been a humble believer in Christ, he could have had such wisdom and power without being turned into a robot.

Practical power comes through the Spirit of God, whose "service is perfect freedom." Mary Slessor showed how to learn from the Spirit as Teacher. Every morning before dawn she would rise and spend an hour or more with her Bible and in prayer. All through the busy day she would keep doing the Lord's work without worry, or hurry, or flurry. Adopting orphan waifs and in many other ways serving as "everybody's mother," this unschooled Scotswoman showed what it meant to "walk in the Spirit" (Gal. 5:25).

My life is one daily, hourly record of answered prayer. For physical health, for mental overstrain, for guidance marvelously given, for errors and dangers averted, for enmity to the Gospel subdued, for help provided at the exact moment needed, for everything that goes to make up my poor service—I can testify that God answers prayer.[6]

Conditions locally may call for a practical sermon about "The Holy Spirit in Your Body." "What? know ye not that your body is the temple of the Holy Ghost?" (I Cor. 6:19).

[4] Visions and Tasks (New York: E. P. Dutton & Co., 1910), "Going Up to Jerusalem," p. 330.
[5] Lectures and Lay Sermons (New York: E. P. Dutton & Co., 1910), p. 340.
[6] W. P. Livingstone, Mary Slessor of Calabar (London: Nisbet & Co., 1916), p. 293.

The introduction may deal with the idea of a temple. Locally this may mean the home sanctuary, but the people ought also to think about a place of worship in Corinth. In that city full of stately edifices with lofty pillars, the most beautiful and imposing structure would be the temple. The sermon proper might have two parts:

I. Your body as a temple of the Holy Spirit
II. Your body to be used for the service of God

The layman should think of his body as the most wonderful thing God has made. Alas, he may have used it as a stable. In Boston during the Revolutionary War, British troops used Old South Meeting House to shelter their horses. Later the church people cleansed those "Augean stables" and restored the building for the worship of God. So the Spirit can transform the body of a drunkard or a harlot, as He does repeatedly through Alcoholics Anonymous and other agencies. Then the custodian of his own body as a temple keeps it as immaculate as if he were in charge of Boston's New Old South Church.

Does this matter seem complicated? If so, the fault is with the statement, not with the plan. It would go on a card three by five inches, and that without crowding. With a simple plan and a heart on fire a minister can preach without notes. Or he may carry them into the pulpit, where he will soon forget his fears and never once look down. Early in a sermon F. W. Robertson used to crumple up his few notes and cast them aside. He could do so because he had in mind a plan of his own making, a plan so simple that he could see each stage at the proper time.

A doctrinal sermon may have too many first-class plans. Starting with the idea of the body as a temple, the sermon may shift to another design equally attractive. "This is my body, which is broken for you" (I Cor. 11:24b). According to a plan that I have borrowed, a person looks on his body in one of three ways:

I. A Christian says to his Lord: "My body for Thee."
II. A "good moral man" says to himself: "My body for me."
III. A wicked man says to his neighbor, a man or a woman: "Thy body for me."

Why arrange the ideas in this order? Because the first comes out of the text, and the other two afford a contrast, with climactic effectiveness. Of the three ideas the third most interests the average man. The climax here is psychological: "Thy body for me." That sounds diabolical, and the devil is always interesting.

This runs counter to what I was taught about starting with the little and building up toward the large. I get my ideas about climax from the Scriptures and from study of master sermons. In the Ten Commandments the First Table comes before the Second. The First is the more important— that is what "first" means in the Bible—but the Second is more interesting. Hence the climax. When our Lord describes religion in terms of love, He follows this order: God first, neighbor second, self last (Matt. 22:36-40). So in the epistles of Paul the doctrine usually precedes the application. The basis is theological, but the climax is psychological. Search the Scriptures and see.

Note also the structure of F. W. Robertson's sermon "The Three Crosses of Calvary" (Luke 23:33). He followed the order of the ideas as they appear in the Scriptures, where the stress falls on the Cross of Christ. Apart from that Cross the other two would not appear. After a contemporary introduction about the solemnity of a dying hour, Robertson dealt first with the Cross of Christ, then with the cross of the impenitent thief, lastly with the cross of the forgiven sinner. That sermon had climax, which lesser men have lost by shifting the order of the three crosses. People ought to be concerned most of all about the dying Redeemer, but the average man finds the facts about the penitent thief climactic.

"Perhaps so, but what about the body as a temple? You have forgotten what you started to say!" No, I have been showing the folly of shifting plans in the middle of a sermon. Each of these ideas—that of the temple, that of the three men, and that of the three crosses—suggests too many ideas for a sermon. Why weaken the temple idea by introducing either or both of the others, even though they all have to do do with a man's body? How can a layman carry away a clear impression of two or three motifs all mixed up in one homiletical mess?

An inspirational preacher can have more than one design for a sermon and still not confuse the hearers. He does not wish to teach, and he does not make structure stand out. But when a doctrinal preacher tries to do more than one thing at a time, he fails to teach. If it were necessary, and kind, I could give examples here of first-class materials practically spoiled by being presented in sermons with multiple plans. So it seems that when a doctrinal preacher has found the right plan for a sermon, he must forsake all others and cleave to this one. Otherwise the people may learn little or nothing, because they have a spendthrift preacher.

HELPING THE HEARER REMEMBER

The right plan for a sermon helps a layman to follow it with ease and remember enough of it to live in its light. With a simple plan the minister can repeat the most important parts at intervals, knowing that the layman will not remember what he hears only once. Without taking time to repeat the salient points, a speaker may paint too many pictures, point out too many trails, ask for too many decisions, sending the hearer away confused about the distinction between the Matterhorn and the Taj Mahal, and wondering what the surmises of the sky pilot have to do with life tomorrow in Cream Ridge or on Broadway.

After an inspirational message a layman may remember nothing, and still feel refreshed. If so, thank God, but a pulpit ought to be more than a refreshment stand. After a doctrinal sermon any hearer ought to know the gist of what has been taught, and how to apply it in his daily living. How then can a pastor make the right plan for a doctrinal sermon, and feel sure that the lay friend will recall something worth remembering and doing? Looking at a completed plan ready for writing out, let us take for granted: (1) A clear statement of purpose, concrete, local, and practical. (2) A text chosen to meet the need in view. (3) A topic showing the meaning of the text in view of the local need. Then what?

1. *The Approach.* Plan the introduction late rather than early, and keep it short. Early you may see a way to begin, but not until you have charted the course can you feel sure that the first idea was the best. In its final form the approach should have to do with the topic as it concerns the hearer right now.

2. *The Big Thing First.* In the home pulpit, when addressing people you know, do not waste a minute getting started. Begin at once to preach your doctrine. In baseball a pitcher does his warming up before he comes to the mound. Homiletically this means to start preaching at once. A preacher

169

elsewhere may have to work otherwise. Those other ways may have their place,[7] but not in a doctrinal sermon.

3. *Parallel Headings.* Master preachers, such as Alexander Maclaren, often arrange sermon headings in parallel form, which helps the layman follow the sermon. Among the plans in this book a person remembers most clearly the one about three men and the body. Why memorable? Because of simplicity, and parallelism. "My body for Thee." "My body for me." "Thy body for me." Of course one cannot do this sort of thing in every sermon. Have variety!

4. *Sentence Headings.* With Maclaren and others parallel headings often appear in declarative sentences, much alike and short. In one of Maclaren's ablest books, *The Secret of Power*, more than half of the twenty sermons have sentence headings, usually four in number. While he did not often stress doctrine, Maclaren knew how to teach. His sentence headings gave a sense of completeness, with an air of authority.

5. *Phrases as Headings.* Many teaching sermons have phrases as headings. On an automobile trip a tourist likes to have road signs simple and all alike. He also likes to have them repeated at intervals. "Pittsburgh, ——— Miles." "St. Louis, ——— Miles." "Denver, ——— Miles." So in charting a doctrinal sermon, have a few road signs easy to follow, and repeat the right one at intervals.

6. *Question Headings.* Old-time preachers often used questions as headings. Anyone can plan a sermon this way in three minutes. "Where Is Pittsburgh?" "How Far to St. Louis?" "When Do We Reach Denver?" This would sound silly anywhere except in a sermon. In a doctrinal message stress answers, not questions.

[7] For inductive preaching see J. Fort Newton, *The New Preaching* (New York and Nashville: Cokesbury Press, 1930), pp. 115-17.

7. *Symmetry of Parts.* As in a first-class novel or drama, the main parts of a sermon ought to run about the same length. Otherwise one part may be overdeveloped, and another part not full enough. Sometimes a man prepares the first part carefully, the second partially, the third scantily. Then he may wonder why the sermon starts to sag when it ought to soar.

8. *Planning for a Climax.* Ideally, each main part should have a climax, with the chief one near the end of the sermon. Near it, but not too near. If the sermon keeps on growing more intense, until it reaches a climactic height near the end, there should be a quieter close, so that the hearer will make the right decision.

9. *Sermon Delivery.* The effect of a doctrinal sermon depends largely on delivery. If the layman is to follow it with ease and remember the gist of it all, the minister should not speak so rapidly as when he wishes to inspire. Nobody but a dunce would keep the same tempo all through a sermon. In general, a man with a teaching message speaks more deliberately than one who inspires. Who can teach while rushing along pell-mell, as to a forest fire?

10. *Pleasing Variety.* All these suggestions give way before the need for variety from sermon to sermon. Also within each one, from stage to stage. Otherwise the romance of preaching may degenerate into the prattling of a parrot, which never changes content, pitch, tempo, or anything else. To insure pleasing variety, let each sermon follow the right plan.

171

CHAPTER FOURTEEN

THE USE OF
ILLUSTRATIONS FROM LIFE

DOCTRINAL PREACHING HAS THE REPUTATION OF seeming dull, heavy, and unreal. It may even consist in "the unilluminating discussion of unreal problems in unintelligible language." To avoid such a travesty, consider what Charles R. Brown calls "the lighter elements of the sermon," notably the illustrations. Any lover of sermons can make a list of preachers who have excelled in the use of illustrations. The list that follows has no special reference to doctrine.

WATCHING THE WAYS OF MASTERS

Our Lord in the parables—Hosea and Amos—John the Baptist and Paul—Chrysostom and Bernard of Clairvaux—Bunyan and Thomas Guthrie—Spurgeon and John McNeill—Joseph Parker and Weatherhead. On our side of the Atlantic, Moody and Talmage—Fosdick and Sockman—Chappell and Macartney—the Luccocks, father and son—with others whom the reader can name. Instead of surveying the field broadly, sit down with the sermons of one man. Better still, take two and contrast their ways of illustrating sermons.

In an educational center James S. Stewart used fresh illustrations, often from books. In a downtown church of a manufacturing city Macartney often drew from American history and biography. In the South, among city people who knew country life, Chappell often referred to boyhood experiences on the farm. No one of these men could have exchanged illustrations with either of the others. Each chose what came out of his own background and interested his hearers. For example, Chappell once showed a congregation what Horace Bushnell had taught in *Christian Nurture.* Without referring to that book, of which his people had never heard, Chappell used a homely illustration.

A farmer gave his little boy a colt the day it was foaled. The lad lived with his colt, "gentled" it, led it to obey, and after a while taught it how to behave under a saddle or in harness. Another colt grew up on the farm, where it ran wild. After three years this colt had to be taken in hand and broken. Both colts became useful horses, though not equally valuable. Which way of rearing a colt, or a child, does God prefer? That of loving or that of breaking? This example I give from memory, having read it once years ago. Best of all, I remember what it illustrated.

No preacher can use too many good illustrations. So declared Henry Sloane Coffin, a teacher of the art of preaching. He must have been thinking about a man's pulpit work over a period of time. Into any single message anyone can crowd too many examples. In this chapter I am doing so. Deliberately, I am breaking all "the rules of the game." As a rule one illustration by itself does more good than two or more running tandem. A poor one may do more harm than good. The meaning of a good illustration appears in one of Coffin's early lectures at Yale. In speaking about "The Ministry of Evangelism," he closed with a personal experience. One day in New York City at the busiest hour he was standing on a corner of Fifth Avenue.

Two long lines of vehicles moving up and two lines moving down the avenue seemed to fill it from curb to curb. There were omnibuses and automobiles with shoppers and pleasure-seekers, delivery wagons and, just in front of me, a United States mail-cart. Suddenly the shrill sound of a fire klaxon was heard, and a hook-and-ladder-motor-truck swung into the avenue, and sped up the hill. As by a miracle the columns of vehicles parted, and in the cleared center the fire-truck ran without a stop up the avenue. Everything was at stake—homes, pleasures, business, government, would be nothng, if the fire got beyond control.

Today our entire civilization is threatened. . . . The Church of Christ which is certain of a salvation, and of only one, need make no apology nor speak hesitantly, but with urgent insistence demand right of way for the Gospel of God.[1]

This example would repay study. Among other things it comes at the end, not the beginning; introduces a well-known person and looks at everything through his eyes; shows busy tides of life on a city street and all at once a change. After an ominous lull, action, swift and sure. Facts, facts, facts! Life, motion, color, plus suspense; and then a sigh of relief. The speaker assumes that the fire has been put out. Only a master could describe such a scene without once "missing fire," to call attention away from the winning of souls.

PREACHING ABOUT CONSCIENCE

After Easter may come a few sermons about conscience. Everyone has a conscience; no one knows what it means. Psychologists seldom deal with the matter. Not so with the Scriptures. They show us practically that conscience means the way God-given powers work in choosing between right and wrong. The Bible stress falls, not on meaning, but on cleansing. In Hebrews an eloquent writer has been discussing Jewish ways of dealing with a conscience defiled. Then he

[1] *In a Day of Social Rebuilding* (New Haven, Conn.: Yale University Press, 1918), p. 81. Used by permission of the publisher.

points to the New Testament way as far better. "How much more shall the blood of Christ . . . purge your conscience from dead works to serve the living God?" (9:14). Topic: "How to Have a Clean Conscience." A problem approach: everyone in church has a conscience and wishes it to be clean. The sermon ought to tell how.

   I. Conscience has to do with right and wrong.
      It shows—urges—approves—rebukes.
  II. Conscience may get foul and work poorly.
 III. Conscience needs to be cleansed at the Cross.

This kind of sermon calls for examples from life. John A. Hutton, Lynn H. Hough, or some other Christian humanist could show that conscience dominates classic literature and art; Greek drama, grand opera, Shakespeare's tragedies, Russian fiction, and other novels such as Hugo's *Les Miserables* and Hawthorne's *Scarlet Letter*. "Literary preaching" delights many of us who love books. It might not interest and help some engineers and others to whom I preach every summer in a well-to-do suburb. According to the *Saturday Review* less than fifty per cent of American adults read books. Most readers know nothing about classics. Bookish illustrations that go well in a university chapel do not mean much in certain other places.

Many hearers feel more concern about practical science. If a minister can talk intelligently about such things, he can illustrate conscience. Think of a burglar alarm on a bank, a warning at a railroad crossing, two crossed bones on a bottle of arsenic, a clinical thermometer, a set of bathroom scales, and so on. One example at a time is enough. These analogies all suffer from the same defect. They make conscience seem mechanical. A workman with a seeing eye and a piece of rag, or a screw driver, can make a machine run smoothly. Not so with a conscience defiled by sin. That calls for cleansing at the Cross.

The best illustrations of New Testament truth come from facts about Old Testament characters, one at a time. But what if the hearer thinks of Sodom and Gomorrah as husband and wife? Even if it comes from the Bible, an illustration that needs to be explained may miss the mark. We should not quit using such examples, but we should use them in such a way as to throw light. If any illustration will not throw light on the truth in hand, out that illustration must go. Illustrations have their being only to promote the welfare of the hearer.

We ought to draw more often from church history. Once a thoughtful layman asked Dean W. L. Sperry, of Harvard Divinity School, if anything had taken place between New Testament days and the Reformation. As a lifelong church-goer the layman had heard nothing of the sort. Probably he did not know the religious history of his own state. At Salem in 1692 Samuel Sewall presided over a special court that condemned nineteen "witches" to death. Afterwards he repented and sought cleansing of conscience through public confession. In Old South Meeting House once a year he stood with bowed head while the minister read Sewall's confession of guilt and plea for pardon. Concerning that confession Whittier wrote:

> Which the good man lifelong kept,
> With a haunting sorrow that never slept.[2]

This example falls short. It does not show peace of conscience through divine pardon and cleansing. For that peace

---

[2] From "The Prophecy of Samuel Sewall."

we may look to Paul. In full view of his part in the lynching of Stephen and in the slaughter of saints who followed Christ, he could write to the Philippians about his peace of heart. Through the Cross he found pardon; from the indwelling Christ he got peace. When once a man has confessed his sin, has made restitution if possible, and has received forgiveness, he ought not to keep on confessing that sin. Forgetting the things behind, let him press forward (Phil. 3:13-14).

My conscience long troubled me about Calvin's condoning the death of Servetus. Now I know what to tell laymen. In 1903, 350 years after that tragedy, followers of Calvin assembled at the scene and dedicated an expiatory monument. Under the leadership of Emile Doumergue, then engaged in publishing his monumental biography of Calvin, those church leaders showed contrition for his sin. These facts come from a Presbyterian historian, who remarks:

The example is to be commended to other branches of the Christian Church. If it were followed, Europe would bristle with expiatory monuments. [America might have some at scenes of Indian massacres, such as Gnadenhutten, Ohio!] But after all it is permitted to ask whether monuments can ever expiate. The deed was done. When all is said, admirers of Calvin must still look back on it with shame.[3]

DEALING WITH PRIVATE PRAYER

In early summer a pastor may speak about prayer. He will find people intensely concerned. One June the minister of the First Baptist Church, Augusta, Georgia, Robert J. Robinson, asked the people to choose from the morning and evening subjects of the past year the two sermons they wished him to

[3] John T. McNeill, *The History and Character of Calvinism* (New York: Oxford University Press, 1954), p. 176.

use on "Preach-It-Again Sunday." From mimeographed sheets containing texts, topics, and brief notes, they chose these subjects: "Does Prayer Work?" and "When the Bible Fails to Speak." From a list not specially doctrinal, they selected two doctrinal subjects, one about prayer. Similar polls elsewhere have shown that people want sermons on doctrine, especially prayer.

A growing denomination, such as the United Church of Canada, may need more recruits for the ministry (Luke 10:2). The best ones come from homes where parents of a newborn boy dedicate him to the service of the Church (I Sam. 1: 27-28). At Cadiz, Ohio, Matthew Simpson's mother was early left a widow. In time he became a physician and gladly assumed her support. When he felt called to the ministry, he hesitated to tell her. At last he did so, and her eyes filled with tears. Then she told the future bishop:

"My son, I have been looking for this hour ever since you were born." She then told me how she and my dying father, who left me an infant, consecrated me to God, and prayed that, if it were his will, I might become a minister. And yet [she] had never dropped a word or intimation in my hearing that she desired me to be a preacher. She believed so fully in a divine call that she thought it wrong to bias the youthful mind with even a suggestion.[4]

An example may enliven a sermon about "The Patience of Unanswered Prayer" (II Cor. 12:8-9). According to an English novel a physician had twin children, Dan and Dinah. When they were eight years of age, the father decided that they ought to sleep in separate rooms and attend different schools. Heartbroken they knelt down to pray that night. Dan

[4] George R. Crooks, *The Life of Bishop Matthew Simpson* (New York: Harper & Bros., 1890), p. 50.

led: "Please, God, You promised in the Prayer Book that where two or three are gathered together, You would grant their request. So please listen to Dinah and me. . . . Dinah wants to be a boy, so that she can go to school with me and do all the things boys do, and I want her to be a boy."

"Amen!" said Dinah, loudly.

Twenty years later Dinah had been married and had become a mother. She often talked with Dan about their childish prayer. They both felt grateful that God had answered No. The very next morning they had felt relieved, partly because of their father, whom they adored. They knew that he had wanted a daughter.

"Silly little donkeys!" said Dinah, now a young matron.

"But the Prayer Book," answered Dan, "says distinctly, 'Where two or three are gathered. . . . Thou wilt hear their requests.' "

"Yes, I know, but I don't think people should have their requests granted if it would do them harm. That's why the Prayer Book goes on to say, 'As may be most expedient to them.' " [5]

As a rule the stress ought to fall on "Answered Prayer." An example comes from a "life situation." In Japan, Kagawa

has so much security inside that he can afford to go without any outside. Alone in his tiny room of the Shinkawa slums, he was awakened one night by a drunk or half-drunk gangster, with sword uplifted. Kagawa got on his knees and bowed his head in prayer, as he awaited the blow. Instead, the man said: "Kagawa, do you love me?" Kagawa answered: "Yes, I do." Soon the man said: "Here's a present," and handed Kagawa the sword.[6]

[5] D. E. Stevenson, *The Young Mrs. Savage* (New York: Rinehart & Co., 1949), pp. 16-18. Used by permission.

[6] Pitirim A. Sorokin, *The Ways and Power of Love* (Boston: Beacon Press, 1954), p. 53. Other such examples appear in this volume.

A missionary sermon calls for factual examples about answered prayer. A former pupil of mine vouches for the following: As missionaries on a South Pacific island, his father and mother invited the parents of their boy students to a feast on Christmas Day. For the major portion of the food the missionaries depended on the monthly boat, but they learned that it would not arrive before Christmas. So they led the boys in praying that God would supply their needs according to His promise (Phil. 4:19). They did not try to dictate how, but left the matter in His hands.

A week before Christmas they found on the beach a whale, which they afterward used to feed the more than three hundred guests. Many of these persons accepted Christ, largely because they knew of that answered prayer. They had never heard of a whale's being cast on that island shore, which extended twelve miles. This whale was stranded on the mission beach, only one hundred yards wide. The answer to prayer came when necessary to promote the work of God (Jas. 5:16b).

SPEAKING ON A SECULAR OCCASION

On an occasion not religious, a minister can use an illustration to help teach a doctrine, indirectly, but never surreptitiously. If he is invited to leave his religion at home and "give the boys a talk full of spice," he can explain that he always speaks as a friend of Christ, a happy friend. If he goes on this basis, he may have time for only one example in a fifteen-minute talk. So he should assure himself about his facts and their freshness. A special occasion does not call for stale chestnuts.

A convention of Boy Scouts will like a talk on "The Glory of Self-Control" (Prov. 16:32). The example may come from teen-age experiences of Bobby Jones, the only golfer who has ever made a "grand slam" by winning in one year all four major championships of the English-speaking world. "In his early years [Bobby] had a keen temper, almost a fiery one. . . . At the age of 14 he was about as fine a golfer as you would care to see. He stood there with only one opponent, himself. From the age of 14 to the age of 21 he fought a long and desperate duel with one R. T. Jones." At last he learned the lesson of self-control. Then he began to win championships. Meanwhile, for seven long, lean years he had not won a single major victory. Still he had kept on. Why should Jones do for golf what many a young fellow will not do for God? [7]

Another occasion may call for facts about a boy named David. Born in Russia, early in life he came with his parents to Brooklyn. There they existed in an apartment that cost nine dollars a month and had no conveniences. At the age of fifteen David went to work full time; eight years later he moved the family into an apartment with steam heat, hot water, and electric lights. When they went away from their former hovel, he said to his mother: "Leave everything here, the furniture, the dishes, everything." He had furnished the new home completely. David never did anything by halves. Later he became known as an electrical wizard and served as president in the Radio Corporation of America. Long before that he honored his father and his mother (Exod. 20:12a).

A yearly convention of insurance men would care to hear about doctors. At the College of Physicians and Surgeons in New York City the class of 1900 numbered 175. At the annual dinner in 1940 the officers discovered that 68 of their classmates had died, 7 during the preceding year. So a dis-

---

[7] See O. B. Keeler, The Bobby Jones Story, ed. Grantland Rice (Atlanta: Tupper & Love, Inc., 1953), p. ix.

tinguished member rose to make a motion: "I propose that we elect a committee whose business it will be to keep this class alive. We are physicians. We have access to the best methods of science, but we are behaving worse than our patients. . . . How many of us have had a physical check-up this past year?" [8]

On a call for a show of hands not one went up, not even his own. A committee was chosen, and the members went to work. Experts in diagnosis found that a famous gall-bladder specialist had gall stones. A "hernia man" was neglecting his hernia. Some who thought they had coronary disorders found they were mistaken. In the next few years, because of remedial measures, the death rate among those doctors dropped to six, five, two, even one (see Luke 4:23a).

Now for a word of warning. Most of us use too many illustrations. As a man gets older, the situation may become acute. When I started work on this book, I asked groups of laymen what I should tell ministers about preaching. Of course I chose men loyal to their home churches and pastors. More often than anything else, I got this advice: "Tell the parsons to cut down on the number of illustrations and to improve the breed." The laymen also insisted that aged and infirm stories be excused from further service, and turned out to graze.

At a conference, if I offer such advice, I get this response: "Doesn't a house need windows?" "Yes, but it has more need of walls." However secular the occasion, a talk ought to include a truth worth carrying home. It is far more important to have a doctrine to teach, indirectly, than a story to illustrate something the hearer will not remember. On the other hand, no

[8] Martin Gumpert, M. D., *You Are Younger Than You Think* (New York: Duell, Sloan & Pearce, Inc., 1944), pp. 3-5.

layman could object to what follows. Here I am indebted to the secretary of the Methodist Temple in the Chicago Loop.

Charles R. Goff became pastor there a number of years ago. Feeling the need of a Christian painting to impress the streams of visitors, he arranged for an interview with Warner Sallman, whose "Head of Christ" now has a place of honor in the Temple. Fifty million copies of that painting have been made elsewhere—more than any other picture, modern or medieval.

When the two men came together, the artist astonished the minister by saying: "I have been waiting all these years to tell you that you gave me that picture. You gave Christ to me." Years before, the minister had delivered at the Y.M.C.A. a number of Bible talks. One of them had caused Sallman to behold a vision. That night while asleep he saw the "Head of Christ." Awaking he made a sketch of what he had seen, and from that drawing he afterward painted the picture.

Praise God for a minister who shows men the face of his Lord! Would that every hearer might thank the minister by saying:

"You gave Christ to me."

CHAPTER FIFTEEN

THE MASTERY OF
A TEACHING STYLE

THE EFFECTIVENESS OF A DOCTRINAL SERMON DE-pends partly on its literary form. This kind of pulpit work declined in public favor, not because of teaching content, but through lack of popular style. If pastors wish to regain the lost ground, they should dress their doctrinal sermons in a style pleasing today. Since we have been following the general course of the Christian Year, we may think about the literary form of sermons on what lies beyond.

LOOKING AT WHAT LIES BEYOND

From Episcopalians and others we learn to use the Advent season in part for messages about the Final Return of our Lord. I employ this term because I have no quarrel with friends who insist that He has already come at Pentecost. Believing as I do that the living Christ is ever with us, by the Spirit, I feel that we ought also to make much of His Final Return. We cannot dodge the many New Testament passages about His Final Appearing. The New Testament says much more about His Return at the end of the present age than about His first coming at the Incarnation. All these terms—"Coming," "Appearance," and "Return"—are full of mystery and wonder.

John Wesley preached about the Final Return. During Lent in 1758 he spoke in Bedford at the opening of the Assizes— "the periodical session of the judges of the High Court of Justice, held in the various counties of England." Wesley felt that jurists and litigants needed to view those proceedings in the white light of eternity. The sermon met with so much favor that it was printed at the request of the High Sheriff and other dignitaries. Text: "We shall all stand before the judgment seat of Christ" (Rom. 14:10). Topic: "The Great Assize."

Wesley began with the occasion, as every "occasional sermon" ought to begin. The introduction, not long, dealt with the solemnity of the occasion, the sublimity of the doctrine, and the way it should impress lovers of justice. "What could strengthen our hands in all that is good, and deter us from all evil, like a strong conviction of this, 'The Judge standeth at the door'; and we are shortly to stand before Him"?

Then comes a preview of the main headings. Headings that stand out like piers of a bridge between time and eternity. Headings easy to see because they come in the order of time.

I. The chief circumstances which will precede our standing before the judgment-seat of Christ.
II. The Judgment itself.
III. A few of the circumstances which will follow it.

No hearer would remember these headings; but everyone would remember the sermon, partly because he had followed the headings. The literary quality appears in a part of the conclusion:

It cannot be long before the Lord will descend with the voice of the archangel, and the trumpet of God; when every one of us shall appear before Him, and give account of his own works. . . . O make proof of His mercy, rather than His justice; of His love, rather than the thunder of His power! He is not far from every one of us; and He is now come, not to condemn, but to save the world. He standeth in the midst! Sinner, doth He not now, even now, knock at the door of thy heart? O that thou mayest know, at least in this thy day, the things that belong unto thy peace! O that ye may now give yourselves to Him who gave Himself for you. . . . ! So shall ye rejoice with exceeding joy in His day, when He cometh in the clouds of heaven.[1]

Among the sermons I have reviewed, few have impressed me more than this one of Wesley's. Often I have read it through and always with awe. In it I find much the same truths as in other sermons of that time, but Wesley makes the doctrine sing. In thought-forms of his day the style accords with the subject, which is sublime. In speaking to men learned in the law, he dares to be clear, but never seems shallow. No hearer could fail to see the truth that shines out and the duty that follows. At the end of such a message a layman ought to whisper: "I see what you see, and I believe what you believe. I am going to do what you bid me do, and in the doing find delight."

STRIVING AFTER CLARITY

In a doctrinal sermon clarity is a *sine qua non*. As Halford E. Luccock would say, now abideth faith, hope, and clarity; and the greatest of these is clarity. If not the greatest, at least the most desirable, in a day when clarity often seems uncommon. In Victorian times, except for Robert Browning, most poets could make their songs clear to the common people. In our day T. S. Eliot, W. H. Auden, and Ezra Pound have much to tell, but not to ordinary men. In music and in art the same holds true. To Albert Einstein as a lover of Bach, Beethoven, and Brahms, the effusions of some modern composers did not make sense. After he had endured a program full of discords close to cacophony, he leaned over to whisper: "This new music sounds silly; it has no soul." He felt the same way about cubist art.

[1] E. H. Sugden, ed., *Wesley's Standard Sermons* (Nashville: Publishing House of the M. E. Church, South), II, 419.

Some theologians have joined "the cult of the obscure." They have much to say, and say it strongly, in writing for one another. As for laymen and many ministers, such writings might almost as well appear in Sanskrit. In the Britain of yesterday, with the exception of Forsyth at times, every one of my favorite doctrinal writers could make himself clear to my mother, or anyone who knew the Lord. Think of A. B. Bruce, R. W. Dale, A. B. Davidson, James Denney, J. O. Dykes, A. M. Fairbairn, Charles Gore, and so on down the alphabet to William Temple. On the contrary, think of living theologians whose writings call for commentaries by younger theologians to tell ministers what the masters mean.

In America two men stand out as the most influential theologians: Paul Tillich and Reinhold Niebuhr. Either can speak and write clearly when he so desires. Tillich does so in his *Systematic Theology* and in most of his published sermons. Niebuhr writes clearly at will and speaks clearly in the pulpit of a university chapel. At times each man's written words prove hard to follow. For instance, readers of *The Nature and Destiny of Man* know what Niebuhr teaches about the nature, but not about the destiny. Such "teaching" seems like "unrealized eschatology." By way of contrast H. H. Rowley makes his position clear:

I do not regard the belief in the Second Advent as a delusion of primitive Christianity, but as something which is inherent in the fundamental Christian beliefs. I would deprecate all attempts to determine when it is to take place, or to define its manner, but it seems to me eminently reasonable to believe that if the Kingdom of God is ever to be realized on earth, Christ will have the supreme place in it.[2]

On the same subject Oscar Cullmann writes clearly in *Le*

---

[2] *The Relevance of Apocalyptic* (New York: Harper & Bros., 1955), p. 148.

retour dé Christ; espérance de l'Église selon de Nouveau Testament (1948). So does Emil Brunner in his *Eternal Hope* (1954). With any of these writers a man may agree or not agree. At least he knows what the author means. In general, a biblical theologian finds it easier to explain things clearly than a philosophical theologian, who proceeds on another basis. But some biblical theologians today cannot even write clearly about the Bible. Personally I sometimes enjoy swimming in deep waters, if not muddy. But I feel sorry for young ministers who read so much obscure theology that their sermons seem muddled, and still sorrier for their hearers who feel doctrinally confused. This applies especially to the Final Return. Our Lord referred in part to clear preaching when He declared: "He that received seed into the good ground is he that heareth the word, and understandeth it" (Matt. 13:23).

The lack of professorial clarity may have come from the "Germanizing" of our divinity schools.[3] If so, we have less to dread from now on, because most young theologians have been schooled elsewhere. To Germany we owe much, theologically, but not in the way of clarity, like that of Macaulay, or Rénan. One German-minded professor even told his students that they must choose between being scholarly and being clear. They may have misunderstood him; but if so, why? On second thought they might have wondered how theologians as diverse as Brunner, Calvin, and Aquinas have managed to be both scholarly and clear.

The following suggestions are for a minister without the brilliance of a Brunner or the ability of a Barth, not to mention Kierkegaard. Strange as it may seem to some writers of

---

[3] Due also to the influence of John Dewey. See Irwin Edman, *John Dewey: His Contribution to the American Tradition* (Indianapolis: Bobbs-Merrill Co., Inc., 1955), p. 24.

books for ministers, these other men read and think. How can one of them make a sermon about the last things clear, not misty or muddy? I mean clear to the sort of people who come to church. As for scholarship that is not the chief end of the Christian ministry or of a theological seminary. Thank God, however, for scholars, who seem all too rare. I have known only a few.

1. *Preach What You Believe*, and believe what you preach. If a minister does not believe what his church teaches on such a vital subject as the Person of our Lord, he should transfer to a group without such a creed. But if a young pastor does not feel able to preach about "communion of saints," he need not feel perturbed. He can deal with other truths until he learns how to make this one glow.

My own hesitations, doctrinally, have had to do with the devil. I believe in his existence as a person with diabolical powers. If I did not, how could I account for two global wars and the dread of a third? Still I never have figured out a fitting reply to a question that once came to me in class. We had been discussing a passage about Satan. One of the men, a Boer from South Africa, did not understand our English idiom. So he asked me, kindly: "You talk about the devil. Is the devil a man like you?"

2. *Preach What You Understand*, and understand what you preach. No one can comprehend all the mystery known as "communion of saints," but a lover of simplicity can make a part of the truth clear and luminous. One Lord's Day in New York City I heard it done. In the morning I went to a beautiful sanctuary with uplifting music and prayers, and an erudite discourse with ponderous philosophical cosmic speculations that put people round me to sleep. In the afternoon, still feeling jaded, I went to the Fifth Avenue Presbyterian

Church and found a large sanctuary filled. We all sat spell-bound during a simple message on "Communion of Saints" (Eph. 3:15). We heard about Christian fellowship with believers there in church, most of whom we had never seen; with others beyond the seven seas, many of them not known by name; and with saints in glory, including those of Bible days. Ever since that mountaintop experience, I have found new satisfaction in this part of the Creed: "I believe in . . . the communion of saints." I still thank John Sutherland Bonnell.

3. *Dare to Be Simple*, but never seem shallow. A master of the king's English can talk about deep things clearly; someone else can make them seem muddy. Do not prate about "The Significance and Implications of Scriptural Eschatology and Apocalyptic Literature." Preach on "Eternal Life: What It Means to Us Now." "This is eternal life, that they know thee the only true God, and Jesus Christ whom thou hast sent" (John 17:3 R.S.V.). In words of your own make clear what you mean by life, and by eternal life, which relates to God, here and hereafter.

Nobody can tell all that these words signify, but anyone properly educated can explain John 17:3 in terms of today. Often in our sermons life means life, and eternal means eternal. As though a preacher could interpret a word by repeating it often, each time a little louder! If a word is not clear, why engage in meaningless repetitions? Neither a parrot's croaking nor a distant echo of a human voice can guide a man lost in a forest and likely to sink in a swamp. As for the meaning of the text, listen to A. J. Gossip. Note the simplicity of his words:

[Eternal life] begins here and now. And one can know and live it in this world. But it comes to its fullness only in the other life. . . . It means and is to know God as he really is; and all that flows from that. For to take in what God is, to grasp something

190

of his unselfishness, his generosity, his patience, his humility, must give one a new standard of measurement, a new sense of values, a new idea of how life should be used. . . . That is eternal life. It is to live after God's way, as life is lived in the eternities.[4]

4. *Plan a Sermon by Paragraphs*, and preach by paragraphs. Short words help, if not childish. So do brief sentences, if not choppy. In present-day English the paragraph serves as the unit of thought. A teaching paragraph may follow a pattern like this: state the idea in a key sentence, preferably short and simple; if necessary, explain the chief term in words of your own; discuss the idea with reference to a person, or persons; if necessary, illustrate; near the close enforce. All this in one paragraph? No; if this one runs much over one hundred words, wind it up. Then make another paragraph with a new key sentence.

In order to make a good paragraph, put yourself in the place of the hearer. In a "train of thought" let each car bear its portion of the load, with a form easy to handle. This way of preparing a sermon leads to clarity, not confusion. On the contrary, as Jowett says about public prayer, "There is nothing more dreadfully unimpressive than . . . a disorderly dance of empty words, going we know not whither."

5. *Keep to One Subject*, and make it stand out. A paragraph may start with a sentence about the speaker. If so, he ought to serve as the dominant subject of every other sentence in the paragraph. If the first sentence has the speaker as subject; the second, the hearer; the third, the topic; the fourth, the text; the fifth, the Saviour; and the sixth, the Father, how can the hearer follow so many subjects? Not only does a good paragraph keep

[4] *The Interpreter's Bible* (New York and Nashville: Abingdon Press, 1952), VIII, 744. Used by permission of the publisher.

191

to the same subject; there is also continuity between sentences. This helps to make possible a "train of thought."

What I am recommending may sound wooden. But not to anyone who studies the paragraphing in the *Atlantic Monthly* or the *Saturday Review*. Writing and speaking by the paragraph, with each unit setting forth a single idea, becomes a matter of habit, almost automatic. The sentences need not look as much alike as pickets in a fence, but they all ought to enclose the same garden plot.

6. *Rely on Repetition*, and repeat what is memorable. Only a fool would repeat everything. Only a dunce would say nothing worth repeating. Among effective preachers to common people in our century, I cannot think of one who has not excelled in meaningful repetition. For example, take Jowett, whose sermons some pundits stigmatized as "thin." Once a brilliant New Testament scholar went to hear Jowett and came away delighted with his mastery "in the fine art of making a little go a long way. . . . If sermons are to be effective with the masses, the points to be made must be few." [5] Skill here consists in saying comparatively few things and repeating them in various ways, memorably.

The world's literature shows the value of repetition. In the noblest of the parables, "The Love of God Our Father" (Luke 15:11-32), the word "father" rings out twelve times. In Paul's chapter about "The Greatness of Christian Love" (I Cor. 13), this idea dominates every part. In Mark Antony's oration over the dead body of his friend Julius Caesar, the stress falls at intervals on ironic words: "honorable men!" Lincoln's Gettysburg Address has sentence after sentence with "dedi-

---

[5] Ned B. Stonehouse, *J. Gresham Machen* (Grand Rapids, Mich.: Wm. B. Eerdmans Publishing Co., 1954), p. 230.

cate," or an equivalent, as the dominant word. If a captious critic excised such repetitions, he would change a masterpiece into something commonplace.

APPEALING TO MEN'S INTERESTS

A doctrinal sermon ought to be as clear as daylight. It should also be as interesting as life, or love. Under God, a sermon exists for the sake of the hearer. It does him no good unless he listens. Even if he hears the words, they do him no good when they make him feel bored. As for the secret, the art of interesting depends on a man's personality. The style is the man. Every master of the spoken word interests others in ways much his own. This art can be neither caught nor taught. Still a few impressions have come through a study of sermons good and bad. "Bad" here means misrepresenting God and the Gospel by making the one seem dull and the other dead.

1. *Preach About Persons*, not abstractions. Like the Master, give the preference to one person. Show a man building a house on a rock as a home for loved ones. No matter how vast the truth in hand, relate it to the hearer and his interests. Apart from persons, divine and human, such doctrines as sin and salvation, the judgment and life everlasting, have no meaning or value. Away from church the hearer thinks much about persons, especially himself. Get him to think more about God and about others. This is the way the masters preach. They may have learned the art by reading the parables. Whoever heard of an impersonal parable?

2. *Show a Person in Action*, or two persons in contrast. The Pharisee and the publican—the rich man and Lazarus—the prodigal and his brother. In "The Parable on Being a Good

Neighbor" (Luke 10:30-37), use a red pencil to underline every word that shows a person in action. Soon the paragraph will become as bright as a bed of salvia. Note these verbs full of action: went down—fell—stripped—wounded—departed—leaving—came down—saw—passed by—looked—passed by—came—saw—had compassion—went—bound up—pouring —set—brought—took care—departed—took out—gave—spendest—repay—showed mercy—do likewise. Words as motion pictures!

3. *Use Live Words*, and make them march. A live word, whether or not figurative, sets forth something to see, to feel, to do, to become. Such words abound in the Psalms, in the parables, and in the writings of Bunyan. The use of live words shows that a man sees what he says. Instead of employing textbook jargon, with ponderous, polysyllabic abstractions ending in -ation, -ology, and -ism, appeal to "eye-gate," and every other entry into the "city of man-soul." For example, in the parable on "A Man's Religion in Terms of Building" (Matt. 7:24-27), count the live words. Out of twenty-eight in all, not ignoring the little fellows, one student counted eleven live words. Such words have hands and feet. They march to hidden music and sing their way into the hearer's soul.

4. *Use Imagination*, but not fancy. Fancy sees what is not there; imagination brings hidden truth to light. Imagination sees a truth in the large and sees it as a whole. The "synthesizing power" enables an artist to look at a hillside and catch a vision he can put on canvas. Michelangelo looked at a piece of marble rejected by others because slender and in it saw his statue of David. This God-given power enables a minister to catch a vision of the life hereafter and then prepare a sermon that will enable the hearer to become a see-er.

TRANSMITTING GOD'S POWER

A doctrinal sermon ought also to transmit the power of God. This ability to transmit power has become known as force, which means effectiveness with common people as hearers. An able young graduate student came to Temple to learn more about preaching. On each Lord's Day, when free, he went to hear a pulpit master, sometimes from across the sea. After hearing the ablest men of our day, he was impressed most of all by their dynamic intensity. Within each man of force there burned a flame that bade fair to consume him if he did not let it out to set other hearts on fire. As with a blowtorch in the hands of a welder, force in the pulpit calls for wisdom and restraint. When the welder starts to work, there can be no lull until he has completed the task with a skill close to perfection.

Every preacher sent from God has force. As James M. Barrie says about a woman's charm, if a preacher has force, he seems to need little else; if he lacks force, nothing can take its place. As for the secret, a part of it appears in a sermon full of Christian mysticism. On July 4th, 1880, Brooks preached in Westminster Abbey. Where another American would have touched on the past history of the two nations, this man with the shepherd heart spoke on "The Candle of the Lord." "The spirit of man is the candle of the Lord." (Prov. 20:27a). This part applies to preaching:

An unlighted candle is standing in the darkness and some one comes to light it. . . . The fire of the Lord [finds] the candle of the Lord, and burns clear and steady, guiding and cheering instead of bewildering and frightening us, just so soon as a man who is obedient to God has begun to catch and manifest His nature. . . . Above all the pictures of life,—of what it means, of what may be made out of it,—there stands out this picture of a human

195

spirit burning with the light of the God whom it obeys, and showing Him to other men.[6]

In the pulpit, force means the outshining of God's presence
in a man's heart. The Fathers called this quality "unction,"
because of its holiness, and "passion," because of its intensity. Here too we stand face to face with mystery, as Moses
stood at the burning bush. There he found that dynamic effectiveness comes through yielding oneself to God. When a
man's heart burns with that flame, he can speak with power.

According to William Sanday, foremost New Testament
scholar of yesterday, "the center of gravity in our Lord's ministry and teaching . . . lay beyond the grave." So if anyone
would keep his pulpit work from seeming eccentric, let him
preach at times about the hereafter. Once Charles R. Brown
heard such a message, which he recalled with satisfaction. Later
he found it in print; then he quoted this part:

We make too much of death. We do not dwell enough on the
soul and its ongoing might. As one sails the beautiful Mediter-
ranean, . . . one shrinks from leaving it. Then, too, the sea itself
contracts toward the west, the shores draw together, and there in
the way of the ongoing mariner are the straits so narrow, so ap-
parently impassable, so like the end.

But as one advances, the illusion vanishes. The straits are
narrow and yet they are wide enough for the mightiest ship. . . .
On past the great rock at the entrance, on through the six-and-
thirty miles of contracted life, . . . your ship goes and out into a
greater sea, the glow of light and lines of fire on the whole distant horizon are the call of love from afar and the tender welcome
home.[7]

---

[6] *The Candle of the Lord and Other Sermons* (New York: E. P. Dutton &
Co., 1910), pp. 1, 5, 19.

[7] *The Art of Preaching*, pp. 127-28. Copyright 1922 by The Macmillan
Co. and used by permission.

CHAPTER SIXTEEN

THE JOYS OF
A DOCTRINAL PREACHER

THE PASTOR WHO PREACHES DOCTRINE SHOULD BE THE happiest man in town. Many of his joys ought to come in the pulpit and in the study. With certain exceptions the ministers I have known, both in person and through books, have enjoyed pulpit and study. Among the exceptions the reasons for lack of delight have sometimes had to do with doctrine. At the age of thirty-four Lloyd C. Douglas wished to demit the ministry. For a time he did so, though the work of the church seemed to be going forward. According to his daughters "he didn't believe what he was preaching, and he didn't know what he believed."

Twenty years later, at fifty-five, Douglas quit preaching and became a professional novelist, to do untold good with his pen. The doctrinal difficulties seem to have decreased; but still he breathed many a sigh of relief: "I am tired of preaching. I have enjoyed my church here [at Montreal] as much as any I have ever had, but I yearn to get away from the everlasting grind of turning out two sermons each week, year after year." [1] In hours of weakness any pastor may feel this way. If the condition becomes chronic, one should thank God for an honorable path of escape to some happy way of serving the Lord. No person should cast a stone at a minister who feels called to do something other than preach. Meanwhile many ex-

---

[1] Dawson and Wilson, *op. cit.*, pp. 72, 250. Used by permission of Houghton Mifflin Co.

pastors long for the erstwhile joy of preparing and preaching "two sermons each week, year after year."

DOING THE WILL OF GOD

Many of the joys come through preaching doctrine. This philosophy of the minister's work appears in the spiritual autobiography of Paul, Second Corinthians. The first seven chapters led A. T. Robertson, the New Testament scholar, to write about *The Glory of the Ministry*, with special reference to preaching of doctrine. The heart of the matter, according to Paul, appears in *Letters to Young Churches*, by J. B. Phillips, a translator who often throws new light on old truths:

This is the ministry of the New Agreement which God in His mercy has given us and nothing can daunt us. We use no hocus-pocus, no clever tricks, no dishonest manipulation of the word of God. We speak the plain truth. . . . For it is Christ Jesus the Lord Whom we preach, not ourselves. . . We now can enlighten men only because we can give them knowledge of the glory of God, as we see it in the face of Jesus Christ (II Cor. 4:1-2, 5-6).[2]

The Apostle found joy in preaching doctrine because to him that meant doing the will of God. He found the answer to an agelong question that stands at the beginning of the Westminster Shorter Catechism: "What is the chief end of man?" Philosophy can put the question, says Alexander Whyte, prince of preachers, but "it is only a theology drawn from the Holy Scripture that can give the answer." It apppears in the Catechism: "Man's chief end is to glorify God, and to enjoy him forever." "The glory of God is when we know what He is. . . . Joy is the purest, the deepest, and most satisfy-

[2] Copyright 1947 by The Macmillan Co. and used by their permission.

ing delight that can possess the heart of man, and the Scriptures continually set forth God as man's highest joy." [3]

As a preacher of doctrine Whyte himself found joy in grappling with the spiritual problems of people, and in solving their problems by interpreting the will of God. Any preacher can taste such delights if he can answer the "Big Questions" today. What Frederick D. Maurice once declared holds true in the ministry now: "No man will be of much use to his generation who does not apply himself mainly to the questions that are agitating those who belong to it." Today our leading men of state, and in other walks of life, insist that the "Big Questions" have to do with theology. Many a man who has won distinction in a secular field looks on the preacher with a feeling close to envy and exclaims: "Thou art come to the kingdom for such a time as this" (Esth. 4:14c).

The joys of a doctrinal preacher come through daily toil in the spirit of prayer. If he is to know the problems that men face today, he must labor as a pastor and counselor. If he is to solve these problems, he must toil in the study, at times seeming to sweat blood. But who else has so many reasons for working overtime without repining? All honor to an engineer or a physician, a farmer or a teacher, who does the will of God! None of them can know the joys of a pastor who devotes his waking hours to the things that matter most, for time and eternity. Here I ought to include the missionary abroad, who employs Christian doctrine in meeting human needs.

A pastor with abiding joys may never become known in the adjoining state. One day we had in our home a young minister and his wife who serve in a church never famous. With his university classmates he might have gone into business, engi-

[3] Alexander Whyte, A Commentary on the Shorter Catechism (Edinburgh: T. & T. Clark, 1909), pp. 1-2.

neering, or medicine, where he would have had secretarial help, a lighter daily load, and a larger bank account. Still he and his wife feel that the Lord has honored him above all his fellows. As a preacher he can apply the truth of God at the grass roots of our so-called civilization. All the "Big Questions" of our day must find their answers in the local community and in the hearts of men and women there. Hence this man finds in the study of doctrine almost as much joy as in preaching it to men who learn the will of God for daily living.

A pastor may miss these joys by dodging his most difficult duties. "When Will Rogers asked the President how he kept fit in a job that had broken Wilson and Harding, Calvin Coolidge replied: 'By avoiding the big problems.'" [4] No wonder the man from Vermont seldom looked happy! No minister wishes to break down under life's load, but anyone would rather do that than fail to declare "all the counsel of God." Before anyone can do so in the pulpit, he must know doctrine for himself and keep doing good among men. "If any man will do his [God's] will, he shall know of the doctrine" (John 7: 17). What a text for a sermon about "The Illumination of Obedience"! What a reason for celebrating Thanksgiving every day!

> Praise ye the Lord, the Almighty, the King of creation!
> O my soul, praise Him, for He is thy health and salvation! . . .
> Hast thou not seen how thy desires e'er have been
> Granted in what He ordaineth?

DRAWING FROM DEEP WELLS

A preacher of doctrine knows the joy of drawing from deep wells. "No experience can be too strange," says John Buchan,

[4] See William Allen White, *Puritan in Babylon: The Story of Calvin Coolidge* (New York: The Macmillan Co., 1938), p. 371.

"and no task too formidable, if a man can link it up with what he knows and loves." In his other books this author shows that enduring delights come through triumphing over difficulties and surmounting obstacles. Buchan says that Douglas H. Haig, British Commander in Chief during World War I, encountered difficulties with military colleagues, with his country's allies, and with the home government. But Haig had "recaptured the religion of his childhood, entering into his work with a covenanting fervor, and a constant sense of the divine foreordering of his life. . . . He had found deep wells from which to draw comfort." [5]

"Deep wells from which to draw comfort"! What a motto for a pastor who would comfort men and women by preaching! To comfort means to strengthen hearts by leading them to accept and do the will of God. This in turn points to preaching from the Bible. "With joy shall ye draw water out of the wells of salvation." (Is. 12:3.) These wells include other visible means of grace, but let us think only about the Book. The preacher who would bring hearers strength and peace amid life's disasters needs to know the Scriptures and how to use them in the pulpit. In drawing from them day after day, he will find increasing joy, provided he knows how to draw. Otherwise, "Sir, thou hast nothing to draw with, and the well is deep" (John 4:11b).

These joys depend in part on what a man believes about the Bible. At divinity school, says A. M. Hunter, a man may have learned how to take Bible books apart, but not how to put them together again and make them live. In theology he may have studied the "fallibility" of the Bible before he considered its inspiration and authority. Some day every minister

---

[5] *Pilgrim's Way* (Boston: Houghton Mifflin Co., 1940), pp. 167, 176.

ought to face all the important questions about the Bible, and decide what to believe about its claims for itself. Such a decision for life does not come ideally early in a seminary course. These matters about the place of Holy Scripture in a man's thinking, says James Denney, ought to come late rather than early. The Bible, first of all, is a means of grace, not a subject for critical dissection. Indeed, it is *the* means of grace.

It must be known and experienced in this character before we can form a doctrine concerning it. . . . It is as we use Scripture, without any presuppositions whatever, that we find it has power to lodge in our minds "Christianity and its doctrines" as being not only generally but divinely true; . . . that God actually speaks to man through the Scriptures, and that man hears the voice and knows it to be God's.[6]

Young minister, live with the Bible for a number of years. Five days in the week, an hour each morning, draw from this well which never runs dry or gets roiled. In the pulpit, in counseling, and in other pastoral work keep drawing water for the sheep. In so doing, after you learn how to draw, you will find increasing joy. You will also discover and accept, I hope, the Bible's teaching about itself. This too will bring a sort of gladness that few find in seminary days, when we sometimes deal with the Book as with a corpse.

My theory of Holy Scripture differs from that of some other men. So highly do I regard these living oracles of God that I go to them for teaching about their revelation, inspiration, and authority. Of course I begin with Christ and look on each part of Holy Writ in light that streams from His Cross and Resurrection glory. With Coleridge I can testify about

[6] *Studies in Theology* (London: Hodder & Stoughton, Ltd., 1895), pp. 202-4.

God's Written Word: "It finds me." Echoing a seeker at a well long ago, I can testify: "Now I believe the Bible, not because my mother has taught so, my professor, or my books, but because I have used it to help people in need, and I have never known it to fail, when I have used it in faith."

My belief does not depend on a few proof texts, but on biblical theology. By this I mean the reverent study of the Bible as it was written, book by book, with the use of these Bible books in the laboratory of human need. I have not learned how to solve all the problems in the Old Testament, or even in the New; but I have found peace and joy in believing that when I understand any portion of Holy Writ, I shall find it profitable, if only as a danger signal pointing men away from some precipice. For example, who understands all about the death of Ananias and Sapphira? (Acts 5:1-11).

Written "at sundry times and in divers manners" (Heb. 1: 1), Holy Scripture claims to be God's message through prophets and apostles of His choosing. As a pastor and a preacher I have found that the theory fits the facts. Not least because of my experience in helping other men, I believe that "holy men of God spake as they were moved by the Holy Ghost" (II Pet. 1:21b). I believe that "all scripture is given by inspiration of God, and is profitable for doctrine, . . . that the man of God may be perfect, throughly furnished unto all good works" (II Tim. 3:16-17). Because I so believe, I find daily joy in drawing from this well of salvation. The joy comes partly from the fact that I can explain my theory of the Bible to any layman or any lad of twelve.

A pastor can also enjoy living with books of theology, and holding fellowship with men who love books worthy of devotion. My awakening to these joys came at least three years too late. After I had been graduated from a seminary, we had in our home for a week an older minister who talked about books of doctrine as freely as other men talk about business and baseball. To him and to others later, who introduced me to learned works from the Continent, I owe more than forty years of joy in reading theology, the more biblical the better. When I began to make ready for this book, I had only to make a study of relevant sermons, and to assure myself that my doctrinal reading was up to date. The reading itself had extended over a lifetime in the ministry. While I know more or less about the early Fathers, I wish that I knew more. That would heighten my joy.

The prospect of such reading, self-imposed, may appall a young pastor. He cannot do it all in a month, or a year. If he works according to a plan, keeping beside him a first-class book of theology, and preserving sensible notes from what he has read, he can gain a working knowledge of the best that has been written about our holy faith. With joy he will keep drawing from these wells of living water, most of which were flowing long before he was born.

SEEING MEN TRANSFORMED

A still more Christlike joy comes through seeing men and women transformed by doctrinal preaching. A minister would not spend long hours with his Bible and other books if he could not use the findings in remaking men. The power to transform comes from God. He has chosen that much of it should come through the preaching of Bible truth. Hence the Apostle writes about the Christian secret of transforming power: "We all, with unveiled face, beholding the glory of the Lord, are being changed into his likeness" (II Cor. 3:18 R.S.V.). The context shows that the Bible serves as the mirror, and that in the hands of a preacher. When God's interpreter uses the Bible aright, he has the joy of seeing ordinary men and women transformed into Christlike husbands and wives, members of the local church, employees and employers, citizens in the community, and seekers of the Kingdom everywhere.

Joys also come through taking a leading part in the transformation of a local church. What does a wide-awake pastor desire for a congregation? That the people trust in Christ as Redeemer and Lord; love to read the Bible and pray, in private and at the family altar; enjoy coming to church, especially for the sacraments; show a spirit of friendliness with one another and with their neighbors, whatever the race, especially with anyone in distress; engage actively in soul winning; strive to make the community an ideal place for boys and girls; show concern for missions and for everything that tends to make the world more Christian; and give liberally for the promotion of all such causes.

At first the list may seem staggering. A minister need set up only one goal at a time. Not being a Lilliputian, he will find more joy in accomplishing something large than in dabbling with many things little. He will see the fulfillment of such dreams among the people if he gives himself wisely to the preaching of doctrine. Under the leadership of a minister with Pauline ideals, the people learn to enjoy a religion they once endured. If at times they tell the pastor that he works too hard, they will understand his saying with Grenfell, the missionary doctor: "Don't pity me! I am having the time of my life!"

A pastor does not experience such delights unless the people begin to be transformed. A friend who supervises several hundred churches told me that in at least half of them the work was not going well. In many a field neither people nor pastor felt happy. Nowhere did the overseer suspect moral delinquency; but often he sensed the need for enriching the soil, always in the spirit of "apostolic optimism." No congregation delights to follow a pastor who feels discouraged, perhaps because he has no program. If so, the enrichment of the soil, locally, may come through the preaching of doctrine, joyously. Not by accident do these words about sowing God's truth lead up to a song about joy at harvest time:

As the rain cometh down, and the snow from heaven, and returneth not thither, but watereth the earth, and maketh it bring forth and bud, that it may give seed to the sower, and bread to the eater: so shall my word be that goeth forth out of my mouth: it shall not return unto me void, but it shall accomplish that which I please, and it shall prosper in the thing whereto I sent it. For ye shall go out with joy (Isa. 55:10-12a).

MAKING THE MOST OF ONESELF

A preacher of Bible doctrine also rejoices in making the most of his God-given powers. From year to year he keeps growing in wisdom and strength, as in favor with God and men. More happy, more radiant, more like his Lord! According to A. B. Bruce, the New Testament scholar, a pastor's effectiveness is largely assured if he wins and deserves a reputation for always looking and acting like a Christian gentleman, with abounding vitality, a cheerful temperament, and a hopeful outlook. This applies especially to the spirit in which he preaches doctrine, with contagious enthusiasm. As he gets older, he ought often to ask: "Am I a more Christlike person and an abler preacher of doctrine than I was ten years ago? If not, why?"

A man of God should make the most of himself for the sake of the Saviour and the people. As a preacher his usefulness depends largely on his personality. Once at the annual Day of Prayer in Princeton Seminary, Robert J. McCracken spoke most helpfully from the words of our Lord: "For their sakes I sanctify myself" (John 17:19a). Without strained exegesis this can be paraphrased: "I make the most of myself." Otherwise, as William James said about a man who lives at loose ends, a minister may employ only 10 per cent of his potential energy. As for the way to deepen and enrich personality, listen again: "Sanctify them through thy truth: thy word is truth" (John 17:17). This points to doctrine as God's way of insuring growth in His chosen ministers.

Guidance about ways and means comes from Sir William Osler, most radiant and influential of all physicians who have written books, at least since "Dr. Luke" wrote the Acts.

Ask any leader in a profession the secret that enables him to accomplish much work and he will answer: "System," or as I shall term it, "Method," the harness without which only the horses of genius travel. . . . Those who are unmethodical never catch up with the day's duties, and worry themselves, their confréres, and their patients.[7]

Think of a pastor who worries a flock he ought to feed! The joy of the Lord ought to be his strength.

Glancing back let us think of these joys as cumulative. By doing the will of God, by drawing from deep wells, by seeing people transformed, and by making the most of himself, God's interpreter should go from strength to strength and from joy to joy. What a beautiful theory! Yes, and a fact of experience, beginning with Paul and the other apostles, confirmed in the history of the Church, and in the life of many a humble doctrinal preacher today. May the number of these joyous inter-

---

[7] *Aequanimitas* (London: Oxford University Press, 1920), p. 35.

preters continue to increase! "Rejoice in the Lord alway: and again I say, Rejoice" (Phil. 4:4).

Here I rest my case, with the plea that the reader lay the whole matter before the Lord in prayer. For the sake of Christ and His Kingdom, for the sake of the home church and community, for the sake of your own growth and happiness, give yourself to the mastery and the preaching of Christian doctrine. Not only will you keep doing the will of God as pastor and preacher, seeing people transformed by the truth that makes men free and strong to serve. You personally will "grow in grace, and in the knowledge of our Lord and Saviour Jesus Christ. To him be glory both now and forever" (II Pet. 3:18). With peace and joy you will often pray as I used to do in the study, while making ready for a sermon full of teaching about Christ:

Take me, Lord, just as I am, only an earthen vessel. Cleanse me by Thy Spirit, if need be through fire. Then fill me and flood me with "the light of the knowledge of the glory of God" in the face of Jesus Christ. In the pulpit and everywhere among people enable me to body forth the blessed light that will lead them in doing Thy holy will on earth as it is done in heaven. Hear me for the sake of Thy dear Son, who alone can be the Way, the Truth, and the Life, both now and forevermore. Amen.

RELATED READINGS

I. THE NEEDS OF CHURCHGOERS

Baillie, D. M. *To Whom Shall We Go?* New York: Chas. Scribner's Sons, 1956. Sermons from Scotland by a master theologian.

Coffin, H. S. *What to Preach.* New York: George H. Doran Co., 1926. A strong teacher. Five lectures. Ch. ii. "Doctrinal Preaching." Able evangelical liberal.

Dodd, C. H. *The Apostolic Preaching.* New York: Harper & Bros., 1949. A N. T. professor deals ably with the kerygma and modern "realized eschatology."

Farmer, H. H. *The Servant of the Word.* New York: Chas. Scribner's Sons, 1942. A theologian writes well about preaching. The better side of Barthianism.

Jackson, E. N. *How to Preach to People's Needs.* New York and Nashville: Abingdon Press, 1956. Welcome stress on the needs of the hearer.

McCracken, R. J. *Questions People Ask.* New York: Harper & Bros., 1951. Sermons by Fosdick's scholarly successor at Riverside Church.

Niebuhr, Reinhold. *Discerning the Signs of the Times.* New York: Chas. Scribner's Sons, 1946. Searching sermons by a leading theologian and university preacher.

Redhead, J. A. *Getting to Know God.* New York and Nashville: Abingdon Press, 1954.

———— *Learning to Have Faith,* New York and Nashville: Abingdon Press, 1955. A pastor. Popular sermons. Stress on daily life.

Sockman, R. W. *How to Believe: The Questions That Challenge Man's Faith Answered in Light of the Apostles' Creed.* New York: Doubleday & Co., 1953. Radio sermons by a gifted "downtown preacher."

Tillich, Paul. *The New Being.* New York: Chas. Scribner's Sons, 1955. Sermons not popular. One of our ablest philosopher-theologians. Profound. Searching.

Weatherspoon, J. B. *Sent Forth to Preach: Studies in Apostolic Preaching.* New York: Harper & Bros., 1954. An able professor. Findings of N. T. scholars.

II. THE RETURN TO DOCTRINAL PREACHING

Brunner, Emil. *The Great Invitation and Other Sermons.* Tr. Harold Knight. Philadelphia: Westminster Press, 1955. Brilliant.

Craig, A. C. *Preaching in a Scientific Age.* New York: Chas. Scribner's Sons, 1954. Able lectures. Stresses apologetic preaching, miracles, criticism, and so on.

Hordern, Wm. *A Layman's Guide to Protestant Theology.* New York: The Macmillan Co., 1955. A needed survey by a young scholar. Recommended for laymen.

Horton, W. M. *Christian Theology: An Ecumenical Approach.* New York: Harper & Bros., 1955. A world survey by an expert surveyor.

Jones, E. D. *The Royalty of the Pulpit.* New York: Harper & Bros., 1951. Fascinating study of the Yale Lectures. Invaluable for reference.

Kennedy, Gerald. *God's Good News.* New York: Harper & Bros., 1955. Preaching materials from selected N. T. books. Much related material. Inspirational.

Kulandran, Sabapathy. *The Message and the Silence of the American Pulpit.* Boston: Pilgrim Press, 1949. Critique by a gifted man from India.

Stewart, J. S. *A Faith to Proclaim.* New York: Chas. Scribner's Sons, 1953. Theory of doctrinal preaching by a gifted preacher-writer.

————. *Heralds of God.* New York: Chas. Scribner's Sons, 1946.

Wallace, R. S. *Many Things in Parables.* New York: Harper & Bros., 1956. From Scotland. Method expository. Stress doctrinal.

Williams, D. D. *What Present-Day Theologians Are Thinking.* New York: Harper & Bros., 1952. Strives to be impartial. Lives up to the title.

IV. THE DOCTRINE IN SOUL-WINNING SERMONS

Blackwood, A. W. *Evangelism in the Home Church.* New York and Nashville: Abingdon Press, 1942.

Bryan, D. C. *Building Church Membership Through Evangelism.* New York and Nashville: Abingdon Press, 1952.

Graham, Billy. *Peace With God.* New York: Doubleday & Co., 1953. Sermons. Directly doctrinal. Older orthodoxy.

Hartt, J. N. *Toward a Theology of Evangelism.* New York and Nashville: Abingdon Press, 1955. In line with my chapter. Stresses doctrine more than preaching. A liberal evangelical.

Kantonen, T. A. *The Theology of Evangelism.* Philadelphia: Muhlenberg Press, 1954. An able Lutheran theologian. Content good; form not popular. Conservative, as I am.

Sangster, W. E. *Let Me Commend*. New York and Nashville: Abingdon Press, 1948. A London pastor.

Sweazey, G. E. *Effective Evangelism*. New York: Harper & Bros., 1953. Practical goals. Popular with ministers and laymen.

Taylor, Vincent. *Doctrine and Evangelism*. Chicago: Alec R. Allenson, Inc., 1953. A strong Wesleyan writer. Stresses doctrine, not preaching. Liberal evangelical.

V. THE DOCTRINE IN PULPIT COUNSELING

Dicks, R. L. *Pastoral Work and Personal Counseling*. Rev. ed. New York: The Macmillan Co., 1949. Helpful guidance from a hospital chaplain with long experience.

Hiltner, Seward. *Pastoral Counseling*. New York and Nashville: Abingdon Press, 1949. Shows the "successful use of concrete and original materials."

Hulme, Wm. E. *How to Start Counseling*. New York and Nashville: Abingdon Press, 1955. Nontechnical. Commended by experts in counseling.

Hutchinson, Paul. "Have We a New Religion?" *Life*, Apr. 11, 1955. The Cult of Reassurance appraised. Well written. Timely.

Johnson, P. E. *The Psychology of Pastoral Care*. New York and Nashville: Abingdon Press, 1953. Probably the best book in its field.

Oates, W. E. *Anxiety in Christian Experience*. Philadelphia: Westminster Press, 1955.

————. *The Christian Pastor*. Philadelphia: Westminster Press, 1951. Both books commended strongly.

Outler, A. C. *Psychotherapy and the Christian Message*. New York: Harper & Bros., 1954. A searching appraisal and critique.

Peale, N. V. *The Power of Positive Thinking*. Englewood Cliffs, N. J.: Prentice-Hall, Inc., 1952. Long a best seller. Calls for study to show what people read. Not an example of "what to preach."

Roberts, D. E. *Psychotherapy and a Christian View of Man*. New York: Chas. Scribner's Sons, 1950. A theologian shows the resemblances and contrasts.

Weatherhead, L. D. *Over His Own Signature*. New York and Nashville: Abingdon Press, 1956. Sermons on vital doctrines. Among his best books of sermons.

————. *Psychology, Religion, and Healing*. Rev. ed. New York and

Nashville: Abingdon Press, 1952. A preacher-writer at home in the three fields. Stresses healing.

VII. THE PREACHING OF DOCTRINE DIRECTLY

Barth, Karl. *The Word of God and the Word of Man*. Tr. Douglas Horton. Boston: Pilgrim Press, 1928. Oracular. Provocative. Should be read by all.

Bright, John. *The Kingdom of God*. New York and Nashville: Abingdon Press, 1953. A popular study in biblical theology. Well planned and written.

Brunner, Emil. *The Christian Doctrine of God*. Philadelphia: Westminster Press, 1950. Brilliant and suggestive.

Craig, S. G. *Christianity Rightly So Called*. Philadelphia: Presbyterian & Reformed Publishing Co., 1946. Older orthodoxy. Clear. Strong.

Ferré, Nels. *The Christian Understanding of God*. New York: Harper & Bros., 1951. A gifted Scandinavian. Advocates "newer ideas." Stimulating.

Forsyth, P. T. *The Cruciality of the Cross*. Chicago: Alec R. Allenson, Inc., 1940.

―――――. *Positive Preaching and the Modern Mind*. Chicago: Alec R. Allenson, Inc., 1949. Two classics.

Jefferson, C. E. *The Minister as Prophet*. New York: Thos. Y. Crowell Co., 1905. Ch. V. "The Place of Dogma in Preaching."

Niebuhr, Reinhold. *The Nature and Destiny of Man*. New York: Chas. Scribner's Sons, 1941-43. 2 vols. Perhaps his ablest work, especially vol. I.

VIII. THE CALL FOR A DOCTRINAL SERIES

Barth, Karl. *Credo*. Tr. J. S. McNab. New York: Chas. Scribner's Sons, 1936. The Apostles' Creed. Original. Epigrammatic. Provocative.

Blackwood, A. W. *Biographical Preaching for Today*. New York and Nashville: Abingdon Press, 1954.

―――――. *Planning a Year's Pulpit Work*. New York and Nashville: Abingdon Press, 1942. The orderly use of the Bible.

Dillistone, F. W. *Jesus Christ and His Cross*. Philadelphia: Westminster Press, 1953. An Anglican scholar imparts his charm to the printed page.

Gibson, G. M. *Planned Preaching*. Philadelphia: Westminster Press, 1954.

―――――. *The Story of the Christian Year*. New York and Nashville: Abingdon Press, 1945. Able teacher. Able books.

Harkness, Georgia. *Understanding the Christian Faith.* New York and Nashville: Abingdon Press, 1947. Clear, interesting, suggestive, helpful. Popular form. An evangelical liberal.

McArthur, A. A. *The Evolution of the Christian Year.* Greenwich, Conn.: Seabury Press, 1955. Scholarly introduction for leaders of nonliturgical worship.

Machen, J. G. *The Christian Faith in the Modern World.* Grand Rapids, Mich.: Wm. B. Eerdmans Publishing Co., 1936. Able radio sermons. Older orthodoxy. Not here combative.

Micklem, Nathaniel. *Ultimate Questions.* New York and Nashville: Abingdon Press, 1955. A strong British scholar and author surveys the basic doctrines. A liberal evangelical.

Quick, O. C. *Doctrines of the Creed.* New York: Chas. Scribner's Sons, 1938. Among many able books about the Creed, some of us like this one best.

Smart, J. D. *The Recovery of Humanity.* Philadelphia: Westminster Press, 1953. Sermons for laymen by a pastor and educator, formerly an editor.

Whale, J. S. *Christian Doctrine.* New York: Cambridge University Press, 1941. British radio sermons. Simple, clear, interesting, without being shallow.

IX. THE CHOICE OF A DOCTRINE TO PREACH

Baillie, D. M. *God Was in Christ.* New York: Chas. Scribner's Sons, 1948. Strong Scottish theology. Well written.

Brunner, Emil. *The Mediator.* Philadelphia: Westminster Press, 1947. One of his earlier books; still helpful and suggestive.

Fairbairn, A. M. *The Place of Christ in Modern Theology.* New York: Chas. Scribner's Sons, 1893. Well written. Deserves to live and be read today.

Mackintosh, H. R. *The Doctrine of the Person of Jesus Christ.* New York: Chas. Scribner's Sons, 1912. Recommended as a textbook, or for use in a pastor's study.

XI. THE MATERIAL FROM RELATED READINGS

Aulén, Gustaf. *The Faith of the Christian Church.* Philadelphia: Muhlenberg Press, 1948. Recommended for Lutherans; helpful survey for all.

Babb, O. J. *The Theology of the Old Testament.* New York and Nashville: Abingdon Press, 1949. Scholarly account. Not difficult for pastors.

Berkhof, Louis. *Systematic Theology*. Grand Rapids, Mich.: Wm. B. Eerdmans Publishing Co., 1946. The older orthodoxy. Contents scholarly; form not popular.

Bibliography of Systematic Theology. Princeton, N. J.: Theological Seminary Library, 1949. Well done. Should be brought up to date and annotated.

Bultmann, Rudolf. *The Theology of the New Testament*. Tr. Kendrick Grobel. New York: Chas. Scribner's Sons, 1951, 1955. 2 vols. Scholarly. Brilliant. Not conservative.

Chafer, L. S. *Systematic Theology*. Wheaton, Ill.: Van Kampen Press, n.d. Older orthodoxy. Strongly premillenarian.

DeWolf, L. H. *A Theology of the Living Church*. New York: Harper & Bros., 1953. A guidebook for students and pastors. Well written. Evangelical liberal.

Nygren, Anders. *Agape and Eros*. Tr. P. S. Watson. Philadelphia: Westminster Press, 1953. A brilliant Scandinavian theologian. One of the most influential modern works.

Rall, H. F. *Religion as Salvation*. New York and Nashville: Abingdon Press, 1953. Selected bibliographies. A wealth of wisdom from a retired professor of theology.

Richardson, Alan, ed. *A Theological Word Book of the Bible*. New York: The Macmillan Co., 1951. Valuable as speedy reference; also for laymen.

Shaw, J. M. *Christian Doctrine*. New York: Philosophical Library, Inc., 1955. Conservative. Readable. Scholarly guidebook.

Temple, Wm. *Nature, Man, and God*. New York: St. Martin's Press, Inc., 1949. Probably the ablest work by a foremost Christian statesman of yesterday.

Tillich, Paul. *Systematic Theology*. University of Chicago Press, 1951. Vol. I. Scholarly liberal. Stresses reason. Not hard to read.

XV. THE MASTERY OF A TEACHING STYLE

Blackwood, A. W. *The Preparation of Sermons*. New York and Nashville: Abingdon Press, 1948. ch. xv, "The Habit of Writing Sermons"; ch. xvi, "The Marks of Effective Style."

Broadus, J. A. *On the Preparation and Delivery of Sermons*. Rev. by J. B. Weatherspoon. New York: Harper & Bros., 1944. Long a classic in the field.

Flesch, Rudolf. *The Art of Plain Talk*. New York: Harper & Bros., 1946. Secular. Abler than his more recent books.

Garvie, A. E. *The Christian Preacher*. New York: Chas. Scribner's Sons, 1921. Able. Helpful.

Highet, Gilbert. *The Art of Teaching*. New York: Alfred A. Knopf, Inc., 1950. The best book of its kind.

Lowrie, Walter. "The Simple Gospel: A Plea to Theologians." *Theology Today*, July, 1950, pp. 159-68. Well done.

Luccock, H. E. *In the Minister's Workshop*. New York and Nashville: Abingdon Press, 1944. A gifted preacher and writer. Many striking ideas and insights.

Phelps, Austin. *The Theory of Preaching*. Grand Rapids, Mich.: Wm. B. Eerdmans Publishing Co., 1947. One of the ablest books in the field.

Sangster, W. E. *The Craft of Sermon Construction*. Philadelphia: Westminster Press, 1951. Interesting counsels from a foremost preacher in London.

XVI. THE JOYS OF A DOCTRINAL PREACHER

Blackwood, A. W. *Pastoral Leadership*. New York and Nashville: Abingdon Press, 1949. Deals with ways of securing time for the reading and study of doctrine.

Calkins, Raymond. *The Romance of the Ministry*. Boston: Pilgrim Press, 1944. The joys of a long pastorate in retrospect. Well written. Inspiring.

Hewitt, A. W. *Highland Shepherds*. New York: Harper & Bros., 1939. The joys of a rural ministry, a work honored of God.

Jowett, J. H. *The Preacher: His Life and Work*. New York: Harper & Bros., 1912. One of the most helpful and inspiring series of Yale Lectures.

Oman, John. *Concerning the Ministry*. New York: Harper & Bros., 1937. A wise book; for example, ch. xiii, "Fixed Convictions and Unchanging Faith."

Rowley, H. H. *The Unity of the Bible*. Philadelphia: Westminster Press, 1955. A British scholar shows the trend toward constructive views of the Bible.

Spann, J. R., ed. *The Ministry*. New York and Nashville: Abingdon Press, 1949. Helpful discussions by church leaders; for example, "His Study," by D. E. Trueblood, pp. 171-79.

Warfield, B. B. *Revelation and Inspiration*. New York: Oxford University Press, 1927. Older orthodoxy. Strong content. Style not especially popular.

TO THE READER

As a student years ago I learned to read and profit from strong books with which I did not agree. In the bibliography above I have included works of various sorts, which I have striven to describe objectively. As for my beliefs, they appear on the preceding pages. I am an advocate of the older orthodoxy, which comes to me from the New Testament through the Reformation. I do not follow any theologian blindly or belligerently; I do not look on any such scholar as inspired and infallible. Least of all do I claim for myself such prerogatives, which I gladly ascribe to the Scriptures (II Tim. 3:15-17), and to them as a means of grace. So I say to the young reader:

Use scholarly works in helping to understand and explain the teachings of the Bible. Study the Book most of all, preferably beginning with the Hebrew and the Greek. Master the Bible as it was written, book by book. Within a book, study each paragraph as the unit. Work always in the spirit of prayer. Through such increasing mastery of biblical theology you will come more and more to look on God in Christ, through the Holy Spirit, as the Final Authority.

"Search the scriptures; for in them ye think ye have eternal life: and they are they which testify of me" (John 5:39).

INDEX OF
PASSAGES FOR PREACHING

INDEX OF
PERSONS AND SUBJECTS

INDEX OF PERSONS AND SUBJECTS